Library of
Davidson College

POLITICAL PARTICIPATION
AND LEARNING

POLITICAL PARTICIPATION AND LEARNING

By

KENNETH P. LANGTON

THE CHRISTOPHER PUBLISHING HOUSE
NORTH QUINCY, MASSACHUSETTS

COPYRIGHT © 1980
BY KENNETH P. LANGTON
Library of Congress Catalog Card Number 79-53715
ISBN: 0—8158—0382—6

PRINTED IN
THE UNITED STATES OF AMERICA

*For Kimber, Jennifer,
Matthew, David, Tom
and Katie*

PREFACE

The focus of this book is on the decision of adults to participate in politics and the learning process that precedes this decision.

During the past fifteen years a rich store of information has developed concerning political learning in childhood and adolescence. Scholars bestowed less attention on adult political learning; the theoretical essays on *Socialization After Childhood* by Orville Brim and Stanton Wheeler remain a standard citation. It also would be an exaggeration to say that we have given much attention to the learning process itself. The focus has been on the *relationships* between taking school courses and students' political information, *correlations* between parents' and children's values and so on.

Finally, many propositions in clinical psychology have had a pervasive influence on the questions about learning and political participation. We frequently assumed that adult participation was significantly influenced by global psychological dispositions which were learned early in life and were relatively stable across different settings. For these theoretical reasons, or the desire to achieve parsimony in the number of predictors and manageability of design, studies of the antecedents of political behavior generally emphasized what people brought to an action situation. The effect of the situation itself, or the possible interaction between situation and disposition, has been ignored empirically.

With these problems in mind we examine in this book the limits of a number of explanations of the decision to participate. These explorations include psychodynamic, situational, personality and interaction-learning models.

Information is drawn from a number of sources; the major one is a sample of young adults (19-23 years), who are members of the attentive public in the United States. Chapters 2 and 3, which examine the influence of early socialization agents, are based on a secondary analysis of data from adults in five different nations.

ACKNOWLEDGMENTS

It is an impossible task to fully realize, much less acknowledge, one's intellectual debts. I will always be indebted to Herbert Hyman whose seminal works awakened my original interest in political learning. More recently, Warren Miller provided the encouragement and necessary intellectual appraisal during the design of this project.

Five students worked closely with this study from the initial design stage to the beginning of the analysis. The continuous intellectual exchange and collaboration with Mike Sahn, Mark Stern, Tom Ringel, John Boshoven and Sylvia Joseph will remain one of the high points of my university teaching career. Paul Shui performed the often difficult role of research assistant with great patience and competence.

The book benefited from the methodological advice of Lutz Erbring, from a continuing dialogue with Robert Friedrich on the murky waters of psychological research, and from the editorial assistance of Sarah Langton. I am especially grateful to Phillip Converse who carefully critiqued the entire manuscript on two separate occasions.

Linda Palsgaard, Sheila Cichocki, Jane Hanson, Eliana Garcia, Katherine Hewitt, Diana Davis and Rita Soenens have cheerfully contributed their typing and assistance.

In addition to the financial assistance of the United States Office of Education, this project was assisted by the Department of Political Science of the University of Michigan and by the Ford Foundation. However, none of the above named individuals or institutions is responsible for my conclusions.

Parts of Chapters 2 and 3 were originally published in the *Western Political Quarterly*.

Kenneth P. Langton
Lima, Peru

CONTENTS

Preface 7
Acknowledgements 9

1. Participation in Politics 17
   Antecedents to Participation
   — *Personality*
   — *Situations*
   — *Cognitive Processing*
   — *Rational Decisions*
   — *Family, School, Job and Psychodynamic Assumptions:*
   What We Shall Be Doing

2. Socialization Agents and Psychodynamic Assumptions 37
   Introduction
   Socialization Agents and National Development
   Variables and Measurements
   Scaling and Method of Analysis

3. Family, School, Job and Political Efficacy 49
   Introduction
   Analysis
   — *Non-linearity*
   Family, School and Job and Efficacy
   — *Relative Effects*
   — *Linear Relations*
   — *National Development and Socialization*
   Implications of Findings For Psychodynamic Assumptions

4. Cognitive Processes and the Inclusion of Situations 65
   — *Pretest*
   — *Test*
   — *Sample Characteristics*
   Cautionary Note
   — *Maximizing Situations*
   — *Minimizing General Political Efficacy*

5. Political Efficacy: Stable Disposition or Changing
   Cognitive Belief 83
   Hypothesis 1
   Hypothesis 2
   Four Predictors of Situational Efficacy

6. Decision to Participate in Politics
   Introduction
   — Methodological Considerations
   *Political Participation: Five Predictors and
      Their Interactions*
   — Cognitive Sensitivity
   — Relative Contribution of Predictors
   Multiple Criterion of Behavior and Other Caveats
   — Unstructured Situations
   Within Situations
   Moderator Variables
   — Sex
   — Priorities and "Rational" Decisions

7. Summary and Conclusions 127
   Psychodynamic
   Situations
   Rational Decisions to Participate
   Cognitive Processing
   Socialization Agents
   Either Personality or Situations?
   — Situations
   — Personality
   Moderator Variables and Social Class
   Organizational Settings and Political Experience

   Bibliography 141
   Index 165

LIST OF ILLUSTRATIONS

TABLES

3.1	Relation Between Participation in School Decision-making and Political Efficacy	53
3.2	Relation Between Participation in Family Decision-making and Political Efficacy	53
3.3	Ranking of Five Countries By Measures of Economic and Social Development	57
3.4	Relation Between Family, School, and Job Participation and Political Efficacy by Developmental Level	58
3.5	D Coefficient (%) Between Job Participation and Political Efficacy, by Education	59
4.1	Comparison of the Political Interest and Participation of the Students with Two Age Groups of a National Sample Who Completed College and Whose Fathers Were Either Professionals, Managers, Officials or Proprietors	73
4.2	Minimizing General Political Efficacy, Comparison of Four Population Groups	77
5.1	Variance in Situational Efficacy by National Situations, General Efficacy, Past Influence of Self in Similar Situations and Past Influence of Others in Similar Situations	94
5.2	Variance in Situational Efficacy by City Situations, General Efficacy, Past Influence of Self in Similar Situations and Past Influence of Others in Similar Situations	95
5.3	Variance in Situational Efficacy by University Situations, General Efficacy, Past Influence of Self in Similar Situations and Past Influence of Others in Similar Situations	96
6.1	Variance in Decision to Participate Explained by Two Versions of General Political Efficacy and Situational Efficacy	101

- 6.2 Variance in Decision to Participate Explained by Situations, Situational Efficacy and General Political Efficacy 102
- 6.3 Variance in Decision to Participate by National Situations, Situational Efficacy, General Efficacy, Past Influence of Self in Similar Situations and Past Influence of Others in Similar Situations 104
- 6.4 Variance in Decision to Participate by City Situations, Situational Efficacy, General Efficacy, Past Influence of Self in Similar Situations and Past Influence of Others in Similar Situations 105
- 6.5 Variance in Decision to Participate by University Situations, Situational Efficacy, General Efficacy, Past Influence of Self in Similar Situations and Past Influence of Others in Similar Situations 106
- 6.6 Variance in Decision to Participate Explained by National Situations, Situational Efficacy, General Efficacy, Prior Situational Participation of Self, Past Influence of Others in Similar Situations 107
- 6.7 Variance in Decision to Participate by City Situations, Situational Efficacy, General Efficacy, Prior Situational Participation of Self, Past Influence of Others in Similar Situations 109
- 6.8 Variance in Decision to Participate by University Situations, Situational Efficacy, General Efficacy, Prior Situational Participation of Self, Past Influence of Others in Similar Situations 110
- 6.9 Variance in Decision to Participate by National Situations, Situational Efficacy, General Efficacy, Past Influence of Others in Similar Situations, and Prior Situational Participation of Self Among Those for Whom the Issues and Politics are Most Central 111
- 6.10 Variance in Decisions to Participate by General Efficacy, Situational Efficacy, Past Influence of Others in Similar Situations and Prior Situational Participation of Self in National Situations 117
- 6.11 Difference Between Men and Women in the Proportion of the Total Explained Variance in the Decision to Participate Associated With Either Situations, Awareness of the Past Influence of Others or Situational Efficacy 119
- 6.12 First Reason Given by People for Their Participation Decision 121
- 6.13 Variance in the Decision to Vote by General Efficacy,

List of Illustrations

	Situational Efficacy and Prior Situational Participation of Self Among Those Who Gave Either Influence, Citizenship Responsibility or Other Reasons for Their Decision	123
7.1	Correlation Between General Political Efficacy and Situational Efficacy Among the Most and Least Politicized	137

FIGURES

1.1		23
2.1	Influence of the Family and Socioeconomic Development	41
3.1	Relations Between Family, School, and Work Group Participation and Political Efficacy in Five Countries	54
4.1		67
5.1	Variation in Percentage Difference in Situational Efficacy by Strategy and Level of Authority	85
5.2	Variation in Percentage Difference in Situational Efficacy at the University Level by Strategy and Past Influence of Self in Similar Situations	89
5.3	Variation in Percentage Difference in Situational Efficacy at the City Level by Strategy and Past Influence of Self in Similar Situations	90
5.4	Variation in Percentage Difference in Situational Efficacy at the National Level by Strategy and Past Influence of Self in Similar Situations	91

Chapter 1

PARTICIPATION IN POLITICS

Why do people participate in politics? The literature on participation covers a broad array of predictors. In reviewing this research, one is frequently struck by the tendency to treat antecedents of participation as discrete and often mutually exclusive variables. This "either-or" tone is most common in research in Psychology on "situations" and "personality" dispositions.[1] Situations (and dispositions) have been incorporated into the research in this volume because they are part of a larger theoretical whole which will assist our understanding of participation. The absence of the situational perspective in most research designs in Political Science, however, has led us to give the situational point-of-view considerable emphasis. Our aim is not to dramatize the controversy in the literature but to examine the limits of theoretically important antecedents to political participation.

At this stage in our research, political scientists are well advised to examine the possibility that an individual brings to a potential action context psychological dispositions and prior situational learning. These influences plus situation specific beliefs combine with the characteristics of the situation to determine whether the individual will participate in politics. The ultimate challenge is to know when and under what conditions each of these predictors has a trivial or powerful impact on political action.

In the following pages we shall (1) focus on personality, situational, cognitive processing, rational decision and psychodynamic explanations of participation, (2) discuss the relation of these predictors to theoretical concerns in Psychology and Political Science and (3) examine empirically the contribution of these different learning and influence processes to our understanding of the decision to participate in politics.

ANTECEDENTS TO PARTICIPATION

Personality:

Clinical psychologists and personality theorists have long pointed to personality dispositions as one of the prime organizers of human behavior. According to the traditional personality model, these global dispositions have a "generalized causal effect" on behavior. That is, they render contextual stimuli "functionally equivalent and cause the individual to behave consistently across many situations."[2] In Social Psychology and Political Science, the "attitude" has been endowed with many of the same global characteristics as has the trait in the field of personality. Students of politics who have been influenced by this tradition emphasize self esteem, ego strength, political efficacy and so on, as important organizers of political behavior. If a person has a strong ego or high efficacy, he will feel more motivated to participate. Since it is frequently assumed that these dispositions are stable across different political contexts, they should serve as excellent guides to political action.

One of the intentions of this book is to test the limits of the proposition that global dispositions common to the literature in political science have a "generalized causal effect" on political participation and lead people to behave consistently across different situations.

The disposition on which we shall focus is political efficacy. According to the early work of Lane, political efficacy is a psychological disposition having two parts. The first is a belief in oneself as politically influential, and the second is the feeling that government authorities are responsive.[3] In their seminal work, Campbell, Gurin and Miller developed a four-to-five item scale that measured a person's sense that he or she could have some "impact" on the political process and the politicians that manage it, that public officials are responsive to demands from "people like me."[4] Part or the whole of this scale has been reproduced in practically all subsequent studies of political efficacy.

We could have chosen any one of a number of global dispositions to guide this analysis, but political efficacy is a worthy candidate for a number of reasons. First, the literature on efficacy is voluminous. It is one of the dispositions most frequently used in the psychological analysis of political behavior. Legions of experts have tried to link it to vote turnout, cynicism, intelligence, trust and general political participation.[5] Students of political socialization have attempted to trace the origins of efficacy back to adolescence and early childhood. The family, school and adult groups all have come in for their share of investigation.[6]

Second, prominent scholars have raised efficacy to the status of a personality disposition. Others implicitly treat it as a relatively stable commodity unresponsive to the pressures of the immediate situation.[7] This view that political confidence is either a part of the personality, a political reflection of a dimension of the personality, or a global attitude, was quite explicit in the earlier work of those individuals who helped shape much of the subsequent inquiry into political efficacy. In *Political Life*, Lane said that political efficacy, or a lack thereof, was an expression in the political sphere of an individual's underlying ego strength.[8]

Campbell and his associates maintained that orientations like political efficacy

> represent highly generalized orientations toward the world of politics and could be expected to remain rather stable over a period of time. In this sense they are approaching 'personality' status.... However, it may be worthwhile to conceive of them as dependent in part on aspects of underlying personality in a more general sense and to seek their roots in fullblown personality terms.[9]

They go on to say that political efficacy is a reflection, in part, of those deeper springs of the personality, that sense of personal effectiveness or ego strength that tells one "how successful he is in transactions with the environment."[10]

After controlling for education and occupation, Jennings and Niemi find consistent (but relatively low) correlations between political efficacy and projected political participation among young adults. They conclude

> (that) the argument—that the degree to which a young person's sense of efficacy leads toward a participative mode is a phenomenon which is both interior and developed by the self—acquires support.[11]

Langton speaks of politicization as the catalyst tying ego strength to political efficacy, while Renshon sees political efficacy springing from the individual's psychological need for personal control.[12] The twin notions, then, that efficacy is a political expression of deep-seated personality traits and/or a relatively stable disposition unresponsive to the demands of the current environment, continue to be a frequent visitor to the literature.[13]

If political efficacy is a global psychological disposition, it should cause situational stimuli to be perceived as functionally equivalent. For example, let us say we are trying to understand why a group of people decide to join a demonstration. People who score high on political efficacy ("A" in Figure 1.1) will feel confident about participating in a variety of action situations, including demonstrations. Thus this general sense of political efficacy should account for a considerable amount of the variance in the decision to demonstrate (Figure 1.1, A-F). In this study we shall (1) estimate the limits of the generalized causal effect of political efficacy under the assumption that it is a psychological disposition and (2) compare its influence with other explanations of the decision to participate.

Situations:

Some psychologists see the situation as a stimulus which provokes a response (decision to participate). Thus the *direct* S-R link between situations and participation (B-F, Figure 1.1) is the focus of attention. Personality, attitudes and cognition are eschewed as "mentalistic" superstructure unnecessary to the prediction of behavior.

Charles Osgood remarks

> "It is one thing to use notions like 'competence,' 'knowledge' and 'rules' as heuristic devices, as sources of hypotheses about performance; it is quite another thing to use them as *explanations* of performance—unless, of course, one is ready to give up his behavioristic moorings entirely in exchange for a frankly dualistic mentalism."[14]

Considerable controversy surrounds the pure "situational" model. Yet it is not difficult to envision the characteristics of the situation influencing the decision to participate. Compare a voting situation with a confrontation. Would we be equally likely to participate in them both? How do we feel about writing letters to political authorities versus petitioning or campaigning? Would we be as prone to join a local petition drive as a national one? Does it make a difference whether we would be acting alone or with others? How much time are we willing to spend? Does voting fit our time schedule better than campaigning? Are we willing to take part in political skirmishes that are likely to cause our arrest? These and many other characteristics of the situation can influence one's decision to participate (B-F). Many *situationalists* do not eschew cognition, but they do question whether personality dimensions exist separate from situations. They argue that students of personality normally base their assessments of the characteristics of a person upon verbal or observed motor behavior.[15] Personality labels are applied to this behavior often without determining how representative this behavior is of the same person in a different context.

There are many reasons why intuition could lead us to assume that trait, type or dispositional labels are generalizable across situations. First there is the "primacy" effect. Once we form a first impression (typing) of an individual, subsequent information, even though inconsistent with the initial judgment, will be perceived to be more consistent than it deserves to be.[16] Second, we carry around with us "implicit personality theories," assumptions about what disposition and behavior go with what other dispositions and behavior.[17] These assumptions lead us to generalize; we assume positive correlations which may not exist. Third, it has been demonstrated that people overattribute the effect of psychological dispositions on behavior while they underestimate the influence of external factors.[18] Finally, our thinking is bound by the words we use. The available vocabulary leads us to view human behavior in dispositional terms. Allport and Odbert identified over 17,000 trait-like words in the English language; but the vocabulary available for specifying situations is meager in comparison.[19]

The preceding discussion suggests another formulation of the role of political efficacy. This new hypothesis maintains that the belief that one has political influence actually changes from one situation to the next, depending on the characteristics of the situation. This notion that dispositions and situations interact is strongly suggested by several studies in psychology which have separated personality differences and situations while registering the significant contribution of their interaction to variance in human behavior.[20]

The possibility of interaction has interesting implications for our treatment of political efficacy as a personality disposition. Let us say we first measure a person's general sense of political efficacy (A) under the assumption that it is a relatively stable disposition. Then we follow him through different situations, each time remeasuring his efficacy (situational efficacy, "C," Figure 1.1). Does efficacy interact with the situation? Is his score on the efficacy measure constant? That is, does (A) equal (C)? If not, what is the contribution of the global personality measure (A), the situation specific measure (C), and the latter's interaction with the situation (BxC) to participation? What is the theoretical significance if global dispositions like efficacy are found to be highly situation-related?

Cognitive Processing Approach:

Political participation may be a mechanistic response to the direct stimulation of the situation (B→F). However, we also seem to carry with us notions of the world which are formed by direct personal experience or what we have heard from others, be it friends or the media.

Let us assume, for example, that a person is concerned about stringent marijuana laws which the City Council is currently considering. He decides to join a demonstration in front of City Hall. Certainly some characteristics of the situation (no police in sight) may have influenced his behavior. But why did he demonstrate without trying other less forceful means of making demands, such as writing a letter to a public official? The reason may be that the demonstrator was convinced from what he had heard about the failure and success of others that letters would have no influence, that you have to apply "pressure" (D→F, Figure 1.1).

On the other hand, the demonstrator may have been personally familiar with pressure tactics since he had participated in an earlier confrontation. He had demonstrated with others in front of the City Council and felt he had been influential. Generalizing from current situational stimuli and past response in a similar situation, he decided to use the same strategy again to influence local officials (E→F).

This perception of similarity between past and current situations is part of a cognitive learning process in which the subject is perceiving the situation, generalizing from past experiences, and making decisions in a system in which the different predictors are interacting. This cognitive process is similar to the stimulus-outcome contingencies in animal learning mentioned by Bolles. Certain stimuli in the present situation act as a cue for the individual. They help shape his expectancy about possible outcomes in the immediate situation based on what he learned before in a similar situation.[21]

It is relatively easy to illustrate the cognitive interaction between past learning (E or D, Figure 1.1), present situation (B), and one's expectancy about outcomes (belief about one's influence in the situation, C) as they shape behavior (situational participation, F). Let us say that an individual is trying to decide how city officials would respond to a proposed political demonstration. In the past, she had joined a peaceful demonstration against the city police (E). She remembers that experience and sees its similarity with the current situation (E-B). The present situation (B) along with her belief that the past action was successful (E) interact with her belief that in the current situation she can again be influential (C).[22] Thus, she joins the demonstration (ExBxC→F).

Participation in Politics

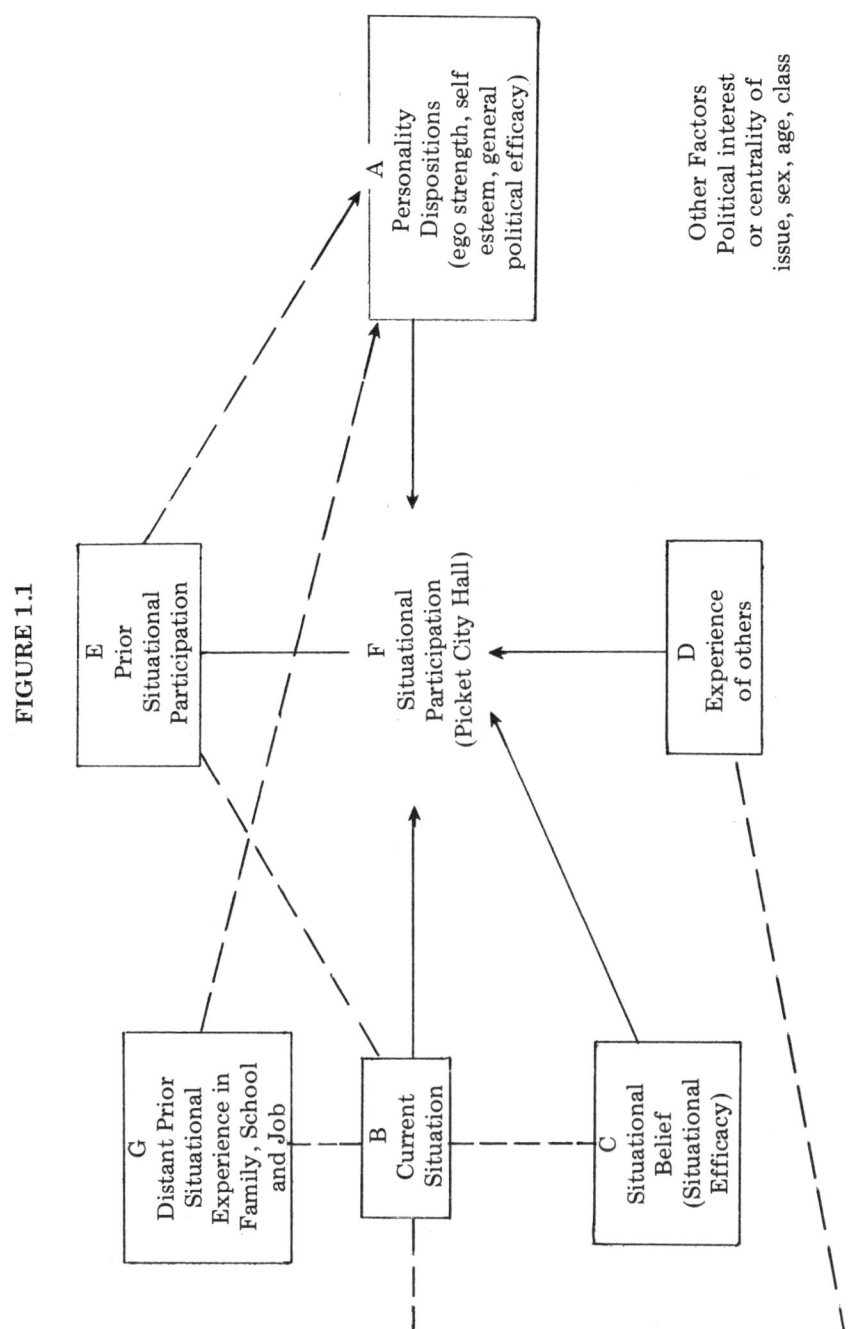

FIGURE 1.1

Interaction between past and current stimuli also applies to what we believe to be the experience of others (D). Suppose a person had never taken part in a demonstration but he had friends who had picketed and were arrested for trespass. When asked to participate in the current demonstration, he sees the similarity between his friends' experience and certain aspects of the present situation (D-B). Therefore, he believes (C) that this strategy is not likely to have much impact on city authorities* and he may even be arrested. He decides not to participate (DxBxC$\not\to$F).

The cognitive processing approach outlined above is more inclusive than the strict situationalist interpretation which would only examine the direct link between the situation and participation (B→F). It also differs from the personality model (A→F) since global attitudes are not assumed to be stable across situations. Instead, this approach is attentive to the possibility that these dispositions are situation-related and frequently interact with past experience.

The foregoing analysis can be usefully applied to "inconsistencies" in the literature and the discovery that political efficacy is often a weak predictor of political behavior. For example, in a useful conceptual discussion Renshon pointed out many apparent inconsistencies in the behavior of those who score low on efficacy scales. Some do not vote and are politically apathetic, while others engage in protest voting and in demonstrations.[23] Nie, Powell, and Prewitt also found in the five nations data that political efficacy was not strongly correlated with political participation.[24] Goldrich** studied the political activity of the poor in Chile and Peru and came to similar conclusions.[25]

The relationship between general efficacy and political participation could be attenuated for two reasons. First, the respondent's history of *past* political participation and *current* feeling of general political efficacy are normally measured in a cross section at one point in time. Yet the causal path is presumed to run from current efficacy (presumed to be stable over time) to future, not past, political participation. Little weight is given to the circularity of effects, that is, past participation experience leading to present states of

---

*Because the object of attention here is a public official, we could refer to efficacy as an attitude. Attitudes toward objects, however, normally imply affect. Your belief that you can have some influence on your Congressman by writing him a letter may involve an affective component (your like or dislike of him), but it may not. It is not difficult to envisage your beliefs about the lack of accessibility of your Congressman influencing your affective feelings towards him, or *vice versa*.

**We shall look more closely at Goldrich's research below.

general efficacy. Second, and more important, the correlation between general efficacy and political participation will be attenuated to the extent that efficacy interacts with situations. That is, general dispositional measures divorced from situations may not be strong predictors of participation.

The usual method of gathering evidence in those cases where inconsistent or weak relations have been found is to administer the standard set of efficacy questions. These measure the subject's *general* sense that political authorities are responsive and that he/she can personally influence these officials. The situational part of the response picture appears, at best, only in such answers as "often," "sometimes," and "never." The questions and answers are typically divorced from the political settings in which the subject may actually find himself, or the different influence strategies that are available to him.

The following illustrates the "inconsistency" problem. Both Jack Jones and Sam Smith scored low on the general efficacy measure. Yet Jones became involved in a political demonstration concerning property taxes while Smith remained politically apathetic. Why the difference? A partial answer may be the relative salience of politics to these two individuals, different feelings of civic duty and so on. Equally important, the finding of an "inconsistency" assumes that each person was exposed to the situation in which Jones made his personal decision to demonstrate. It also assumes that in this decisional context the efficacy of Jones was still low. That is, it assumes that the global sense of political efficacy that Jones brought to this situation reflects a stable psychological disposition which is not reactive to situational stimuli. Therefore, his low general efficacy score should dissuade him from participating.

It is entirely possible that Jones felt very deeply about high property taxes. He had learned from past experience that writing letters to city officials was useless. Neighbors were suggesting a different strategy, however; picketing city hall. This was a familiar situation for Jones since he had once before joined a small demonstration. The street in front of his home had been badly in need of repair. When telephone calls and letters failed, he and a few others had assembled in front of his city councilman's home. The next week the potholes in the street were paved. Remembering the effectiveness of this past experience, he believed it might work again. Jones decided to join the demonstration against high property taxes.[26]

To summarize Jones' case, if political efficacy is generalizable across situations, a general measure of Jones' political efficacy in time 1 should predict his confidence in the effectiveness of demonstration (and his decision to participate) in time 2. That is, a general measure of efficacy is a good predictor of *situational efficacy* (Figure 1.1, A→C). Clearly, Jones' low general efficacy score was not a good predictor of his political confidence about this demonstration as a means of pressuring city officials, nor did it predict his participation. It did predict well his beliefs about letter writing. Jones' political confidence, then, varied with the type of situation in which he found himself.[27] That is, it changed with the strategy available to him, presence of supportive friends, and other characteristics of the situation.[28]

To further illustrate the conceptual utility of a cognitive processing framework in explaining an inconsistency between political efficacy and participation, we shall return to Goldrich's thoughtful article on slum dwellers (pobladores) in Chile and Peru. He asks why these poor people, who might be expected to have low political efficacy, engaged in the political act of seizing land at some risk to their well-being. His study can be interpreted as another example, along with Nie, Powell and Prewitt,[29] of how people through involvement in organizations (situations) may act politically, even though they lack the "psychological base" or political self confidence normally considered necessary for political participation.

However, the seizure of land on which to build houses, and the pobladores' decision to commit this act, can be recreated and explained without theoretically excluding efficacy or the organizational context (situation). Goldrich provides the cue here, when he speaks of the extraordinary amount of political learning that is evoked when the mass public comes in contact with organizations designed to channel its behavior. Typically the pobladores were contacted* individually or in their family dwelling places** by young organizers, often students from the political left. Their immediate objective was to organize the pobladores so that they could secure or seize land for homes. Even though these marginal people shared a desperate need for housing, they often met the first inquiry with silence, indifference mixed with fear. No doubt if a standard political efficacy scale were administered to the pobladores before the first contact (time 1), they would have scored universally low. Few if any strategies at that time would have seemed effective in stirring authorities to respond to their housing needs. The relation between the general efficacy score and their subsequent seizure of land (situ-

---

*The following discussion will apply only to Santiago, Chile, since I am more familiar with mobilizations in this area.
**A shanty or overcrowded apartment.

Participation in Politics

ational participation, F, Figure 1.1) would have been weak. A few of the poor, however, were more receptive. They had had a successful experience with a land seizure (E), but they were now down on their luck and without adequate housing. Their prior learning may have led them directly to the decision to participate in this land seizure (E-F).

For others there was a complex set of interactions leading to the decision to participate. The poblador with past experience (E), found himself again in a setting in which the same strategy was being considered (B). He remembered his past experience *and* saw its similarity to the current situation.

These two factors interacted with his sense of "situational efficacy" (C). Again, he felt there might be a favorable response from the authorities (he would not be killed or forceably driven off the land) if he were to seize land, so later he decided to join the action (ExBxC→F). Those who had a bad prior experience, and recognized the same potential debacle in the pleas of the organizers (E-B), would not have felt particularly efficacious. Thus, they would not participate in this situation (ExBxC↛F).

Most pobladores would not have had prior experience with this type of strategy (land seizure), but some may have heard others speak of such acts (D). A poblador who had learned about someone else's success might have recognized that this situation was similar. This recognition would shape his current expectancy and, thus, he would join the seizure (DxBxC→F). By contrast, if he knew someone who tried to seize land and was shot or jailed, he would not greet the organizers with great enthusiasm.

The organizers were persistent, however. If they had difficulty persuading those with bad previous experiences, they continued to encourage the others. Those who feared reprisal were told about successful land seizures. In some cases the pobladores were trucked to other land settlements to talk with those who had seized land. On some occasions dry runs were held. Groups of pobladores were taken to rural areas where, at the crack of dawn, they would race onto a vacant field with their pieces of tin roofing, boards and tents.

Defense perimeters were set up, soup kitchens and first aid stations were manned. These exercises helped encourage those who were still reluctant to join. Finally the day of the seizure arrived. A sizeable number of poor had been converted by this time from a low state of situational efficacy, to the belief that authorities were likely to respond "favorably" to such an act. Thus general efficacy (time 1) would not predict well their new situation efficacy in time 2 (A-C, Figure 1.1). Of course, others remained unconvinced and they dropped out of the mobilization. As the seizure began, the organizational effort had raised the confidence of the pobladores to the point that they were now ready to participate (BxC→F). A few still felt no more efficacious than before, but they had wives or relatives who wanted to join in. They were ashamed to back out. Thus, even though their situational efficacy (C) remained unchanged (A-C might be highly correlated), they were dragged along by the others. The behavior of this smaller group might be best predicted by the direct path (B-F) which excludes situational efficacy.

Figure 1.1 is an oversimplification of the stimuli that bombard one in such situations. Yet it does suggest five primary factors which can directly influence participation, as well as a series of interactions predictive of the decision to participate. In the case of the Chilean pobladores, situations which combine an appropriate strategy and sufficient organizational support can be powerful stimulants. At the same time, global dispositions such as political efficacy may be poor direct predictors of participation. It is possible, however, that political confidence could interact with situations and past learning to affect the decision to participate.

Rational Decisions to Participate:

One view of the decision process gives considerable emphasis to the role of situational efficacy (C), and its interaction with the situation. The assumption is that people decide to participate after calculating their possible influence in each situation. Let us assume, again, that a potential demonstrator is approached by friends who ask him to join a demonstration at city hall. Because he is interested in the issue in question, he looks at the characteristics of the situation ("B": demonstration strategy, supportive friends, likelihood of arrest or injury, etc.). He tries to calculate how probable it is that demonstrating will influence these local officials, and at what cost.

Typically, citizens do not have sufficient information to make purely rational decisions. Yet if they are calculating their advantage in political situations, this should be reflected in the interaction of the characteristics of the situation and situational efficacy (C) as they combine to predict the decision to participate (BxC→F).

*More Distant Settings: Family, School, Job
and Psychodynamic Assumptions:*

It is generally assumed that parents' treatment of their children may affect the behavior of the children when they are adults. For example, children who have authoritarian parents, who are never allowed to have their say in family decisions affecting themselves, will learn that the family is an important setting where they do not have influence. Suppose the same thing happens to them when they go to school, or later in their jobs. They will learn from these experiences that other attempts to express themselves, in politics for example, are not likely to be effective.

Under one set of assumptions, then, people who developed weak political confidence in early "non-political" settings carry this belief into current action situations. Here they treat the different contexts as functionally equivalent. That is, these people believe that they will have no influence, no matter what the strategy or which public officials are involved. Therefore they decide not to participate.

There are actually two broad views on the link between early learning, psychological dispositions like political efficacy, and behavior. We shall refer to them as psychodynamic and cognitive. The psychodynamic tradition has its roots both in the early clinical study of the emotionally maladjusted as well as the more recent work of the personalogists which emphasizes the quantification of personality dispositions. Common to both traditions is the focus on personality as being composed of relatively stable psychological dispositions which are decisively formed during the early years of life.

Political socialization research which examines the influences of agents frequently adopts this *psychodynamic model* (Figure 1.1, G→A→F). Learning in the family of origin (G) creates stable personality or attitudinal dispositions such as political efficacy (A). This global disposition causes the adult to behave in a consistent and predictable manner (F). Although this is the model, the final link between personality and behavior is normally assumed rather than demonstrated in socialization research.

There are four points, then, where the psychodynamic model must be corroborated. First, one must demonstrate that early learning in the family has a significant impact on adult dispositions (G→A). Second, personality dispositions or attitudes should be relatively stable across the life cycle. Third, these global indicators should not vary greatly from one situation to the next. And finally, these psychological dispositions must cause people to act in predictable ways (A→F).

Even if the psychodynamic model should fail on the third and fourth points (little personality stability and poor predictability), it would *not* exclude the formative influence of the family on later decisions of adults to participate in politics. The new focus, however, would be on how humans cognitively process and organize stimuli. One's experience with an arbitrary parent can be viewed as a small subset of one's past situational experience which may or may not have current political relevance. Adults will generalize from these past situations if they have not forgotten them and if the current context is sufficiently similar.

From this cognitive perspective, then, there is nothing automatic about the effect of early learning on adult decisions to participate. Nor does early learning necessarily influence participation through personality formation. Instead, stimuli in the current situation are judged by their similarity to stimuli in past (family) situations to which a response has been learned (G-B). This chain of events, which culminates in the participation decision, reflects cognitive more than psychodynamic processes.

WHAT WE SHALL BE DOING

Figure 1.1 specifies six sets of predictors of participation. Starting with the most distant experiences first, Chapters 2 and 3 investigate the influence of participation in the family, school and work group (G) upon the development of political efficacy (A), the first link in the psychodynamic model (G→A→F). Two other concerns are also raised. What are the implications of nonlinear effects for the psychodynamic model? Does the influence of the family, school and work group change as nations develop socially and economically? If so, how does this reflect psychodynamic assumptions?

After examining the first stages of the psychodynamic model and the process by which early learning is linked to adult efficacy, Chapter 4 presents a research design in which personality, situations and the other predictors in Figure 1.1 can be incorporated and tested within one framework. The results of this test are presented in Chapters 5 and 6.

Chapter 5 focuses on the third link in the psychodynamic model, the assumption that psychological dispositions (such as political efficacy) are stable reflections of the psyche. If this is the case, a prior measure of this personality factor in an adult should be a strong predictor of his efficacy measured in different political situations in which the *same person* is trying to decide whether to participate in politics.

Chapter 6 examines the impact of personality on the decision to participate (A−F), the last link in the psychodynamic model. This is done within a cognitive-interaction framework which explores the combined and separate influence of efficacy as a personality factor

(Figure 1.1, A), efficacy as a situational belief (C), situations (B), prior experience of self (E), and what we learn from others (D), on the decision to vote, campaign, write letters to politicians, petition and engage in political demonstrations (F). Sex and individual differences in perceptions of the situation are analyzed as moderator variables.

Chapter 7 concludes the data analysis. It compares the impact of psychodynamic, situational, rational decision, personality and cognitive processes on the decision to participate. The implications these findings have for theoretical concerns in psychology and political science are discussed.

FOOTNOTES AND REFERENCES

[1] For a discussion of the "debate" see Walter Mischel, "Toward a Cognitive Social Learning Reconceptualization of Personality," *Psychological Review* 80 (July, 1972), 255; Henry Alker, "Is Personality Situationally Specific or Intrapsychically Consistent," *Journal of Personality* 40 (1972), 1-16; and Kenneth Bowers, "Situationism in Psychology, An Analysis and Critique," *Psychological Review* 80 (September, 1973), 307-336.

[2] Mischel, *ibid.*, 264. Also see Walter Mischel, *Personality and Assessment* (New York: John Wiley and Sons, 1968); _____ _____, "Continuity and Change in Personality," *American Psychologist* 24 (1969), 1012-1018.

[3] Robert E. Lane, *Political Life: Why and How People Get Involved in Politics* (Glencoe, Illinois: Free Press, 1959), 147-155.

[4] Angus Campbell, Gerald Gurin and Warren Miller, *The Voter Decides* (Evanston, Illinois: Row, Peterson, 1954), 187-199.

[5] See Angus Campbell, Philip Converse, Warren Miller and Donald Stokes, *The American Voter* (New York: John Wiley and Sons, 1960), 104-105; Lester Milbrath, *Political Participation* (Chicago: Rand McNally, 1965), 56-57; Meredith W. Watts, "Efficacy, Trust and Commitment to the Political Process," *Social Science Quarterly* 54 (December, 1973), 623-631; Elliot White, "Intelligence and Sense of Political Efficacy in Children," *Journal of Politics* 30 (August, 1968), 710-732; Schley Lyons, "The Political Socialization of Ghetto Children: Efficacy and Cynicism," *Journal of Politics* 32 (1970), 288-304.

[6] Gabriel Almond and Sidney Verba, *The Civic Culture* (Princeton: Princeton University Press, 1963), Chap. 12; Kenneth Langton,

Political Socialization (New York: Oxford University Press, 1969); David Easton and Jack Dennis, "The Child's Acquisition of Regime Norms: Political Efficacy," *American Political Science Review* 61 (March, 1967), 25-38; M. Kent Jennings and Richard Niemi, *The Political Character of Adolescence* (Princeton: Princeton University Press, 1974), 124-132; Christine Bennett Button, "Political Education for Minority Groups," in Richard Niemi (ed.), *The Politics of Future Citizens* (San Francisco: Jossey Bass, 1974), 167-198; and Paul R. Abramson, *The Political Socialization of Black Americans* (New York: Free Press, 1977).

[7] Efficacy has also been conceived of as a norm (one should be politically confident) and a behavior.

[8] Lane, *op. cit.*, 149.

[9] Angus Campbell, et al., *The American Voter, op. cit.*, 516.

[10] *Ibid.*, 517.

[11] Jennings and Niemi, *op. cit.*, 135.

[12] Langton, *op. cit.*, 142-143, and Stanley Renshon, "The Psychological Origins of Political Efficacy: The Need for Personal Control," paper delivered at 1972 Annual Meeting of the American Political Science Association, Washington, D.C. For related literature see Paul Abramson, "Political Efficacy and Political Trust among Black School Children: Two Explanations," *Journal of Politics* 34 (November, 1972), 1243-1275; Fred Greenstein, *Personality and Politics* (Chicago: Markham, 1969); Fred Greenstein and Nelson Polsby (eds.), *Handbook of Political Science* (Reading, Mass.: Addison-Wesley, 1975), Vol. 2, Chap. 1.

[13] Beyond its assumed importance as a global disposition compelling people toward or away from political participation, efficacy has achieved importance for other reasons as well. We link efficacy to the support a person directs toward political authority as well as the legitimacy with which the political system is held. Easton and Dennis, *op. cit.*, and Almond and Verba, *The Civic Culture, op. cit.*, 230-231, 239-252.

Finally, instead of focusing on how such dispositions affect participation or the functioning of the political system, we could look at the needs of individuals. The learning of political confidence may be inextricably bound to a person's own idiosyncratic sense of contentment. The orientation of this book, however, is toward the antecedents of participation rather than the importance of these antecedents themselves for the psychic well-being of the individual. David Sears, "Book Review," *Midwest Journal of Political Science* 15 (February, 1971), 156. Also see M. Brewster Smith, "Competence and Socialization," in John A. Clausen (ed.), *Socialization and Soci-*

ety (Boston: Little, Brown, 1968), 271-320; and Jennings and Niemi, *op. cit.*, 13-15.

[14] Charles E. Osgood, "Toward a Wedding of Insufficiencies," in T. Dixon and D. Horton (eds.), *Verbal Behavior and General Behavior Theory* (Englewood Cliffs, New Jersey: Prentice-Hall, 1968), 505.

[15] Psychological dispositions and attitudes are conceptual constructs which are normally inferred from verbal behavior (interviews), written behavior (questionnaires), observations of other motor behavior, or some combination of the above. Thus, the hatched lines in the figure below represent unobserved conceptual paths.

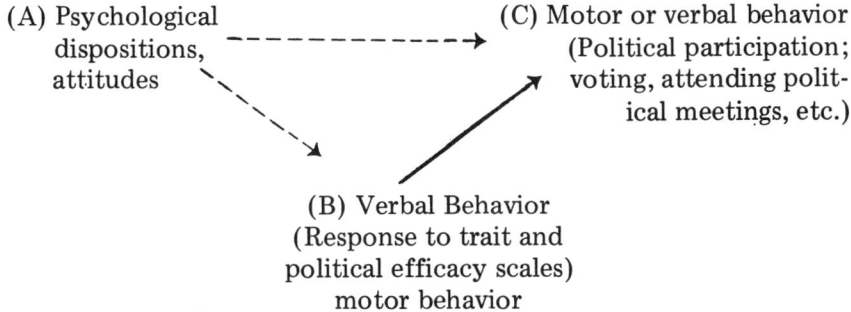

(A) Psychological dispositions, attitudes

(C) Motor or verbal behavior (Political participation; voting, attending political meetings, etc.)

(B) Verbal Behavior (Response to trait and political efficacy scales) motor behavior

The only empirical relationship in this case is between B and C. See M. L. Defleur and F. R. Westie, "Verbal Attitudes and Overt Acts," *American Sociological Review* 23 (December, 1958), 667-673 and _____ "Attitude as a Scientific Concept," *Social Forces* 42 (October, 1963), 17-31.

[16] Edward Jones and George Goethals, *Order Effects in Impression Formation: Attribution Context and the Nature of the Entity* (New York: General Learning Press, 1971). Bem and Allen summarize many of the "errors" discussed here as well as others. Daryl Bem and Andrea Allen, "On Predicting Some of the People Some of the Time: The Search for Cross-Situational Consistencies in Behavior," *Psychological Review* 81 (November, 1974), 508.

[17] David J. Schneider, "Implicit Personality Theory: A Review," *Psychological Bulletin* 79 (May, 1973), 294, 309.

[18] For research on attribution theory see Edward Jones and Richard Nisbett, *The Actor and Observer: Divergent Perceptions of the Causes of Behavior* (New York: General Learning Press, 1971).

[19] Gordon Allport and Henry Odbert, "Trait Names: A Psycholexical Study," *Psychological Monographs* 47, No. 1 (1936), entire issue.

[20] H. Rausch, I. Farbman and L. Llewellyn, "Person, Setting and

Change in Social Interaction: II. A Normal Control Study," *Human Relations* 13 (1960), 305-332; Norman Endler, J. Mc V. Hunt, and A. Rosenstein, "An S-R Inventory of Anxiousness," *Psychological Monographs* 76, No. 536 (1962), entire issue; N. Endler and J. Mc V. Hunt, "Sources of Behavioral Variance as Measured by the S-R Inventory of Anxiousness," *Psychological Bulletin* 65 (June, 1966), 336-346; Endler and Hunt, "S-R Inventories of Hostility and Comparisons of the Proportions of Variance from Persons, Responses, and Situations for Hostility and Anxiousness," *Journal of Personality and Social Psychology* 9 (August, 1968), 309-315; Endler and Hunt, "Generalizability of Contributions from Sources of Variance in the S-R Inventories of Anxiousness," *Journal of Personality* 37 (March, 1969), 1-24; Rudolph Moos, "Situational Analysis of a Therapeutic Community Milieu," *Journal of Abnormal Psychology* 73 (February, 1968), 49-61; M. Argyle and B. Little, "Do Personality Traits Apply to Social Behavior?," *Journal of Theory of Social Behavior* 2 (1972), 1-35; David Magnusson and Bo Ekehammar, "Anxiety Profiles Based on Both Situational and Response Factors," *Multivariate Behavioral Research* 10 (January, 1975), 27-43; and Norman Endler, "The Case for Person-Situation Interactions," *Canadian Psychological Review* 16 (January, 1975), 12-21.

There is also considerable literature in social psychology which examines attitude-behavior congruence in different situations. See Richard LaPiere, "Attitudes Versus Actions," *Social Forces* 13 (1934), 230-237; I. Ajzen and M. Fishbein, "The Prediction of Behavioral Intentions in a Choice Situation," *Journal of Experimental Social Psychology* 5 (October, 1969), 400-416; Lyle Warner and M. Defleur, "Attitude as an Interactional Concept: Social Constraint and Social Distance as Intervening Variables Between Attitudes and Action," *American Sociological Review* 34 (April, 1967), 153-169; A. Weinstein, "Predicting Behavior from Attitudes," *Public Opinion Quarterly* 36 (Fall, 1972), 355-360; Frank Scioli, Jr. and James Dyson, "Attitude-Behavior Congruence in Varying Situational Environments," *Experimental Study of Politics* 2 (March, 1973), 39-60; Alan E. Liska, "Emergent Issues in the Attitude-Behavior Consistency Controversy," *American Sociological Review* 39 (April, 1974), 261-272; and Howard Schuman and Michael P. Johnson, "Attitudes and Behavior," *Annual Review of Sociology* 2 (1976), 161-207.

[21] Robert C. Bolles, "Reinforcement, Expectancy, and Learning," *Psychological Review* 79 (September, 1972), 394-409.

In Chapters 6 and 7 we shall examine some of the personal factors which affect the cognitive activity by which individuals associate stimuli with outcomes.

²² Some scholars maintain that a cognitive process is associated with feelings of political competence and add political interest and awareness questions to their indices. The illustration in the text suggests that the belief itself—that officials can be influenced and will respond—has an important cognitive component based on past personal experience or awareness of the experience of others. See Samuel Barnes, "Leadership Style and Political Competence," in Lewis Edinger (ed.), *Political Leadership in Industrialized Societies* (New York: John Wiley and Sons, 1967), 60, and Edward Muller, "Cross-National Dimensions of Political Competence," *American Political Science Review* 64 (September, 1970), 782-809.

²³ Renshon, *op. cit.*, 3. Also see Donald T. Campbell, "Social Attitudes and Other Acquired Dispositions," in Sigmund Koch (ed.), *Psychology: A Study of Science*, Vol. 6 (McGraw Hill, 1964), 159-162.

²⁴ The political efficacy measure used in their study was conceptually similar to the standard political efficacy construct. When the dependent variable, political participation, was disaggregated into more active behavior (contacting public officials) and talking politics with acquaintances, the direct path between efficacy and contacting local officials was stronger than for the other five predictors in three of the five countries. However, it never was greater than .23 in any country. Norman Nie, G. Bingham Powell Jr., and Kenneth Prewitt, "Social Structure and Political Participation: Developmental Relationships," *American Political Science Review* 63 (1969), Parts 1 and 2, 377, 816, 830.

²⁵ Daniel Goldrich, "Political Organization and the Politicization of the Poblador," *Comparative Political Studies* 3 (July, 1970), 176-202. On the other hand, the authors of *The American Voter* reported a 39 percent difference in voting turnout between those who score high and low in political efficacy. They did not report how much variance in turnout was accounted for by general efficacy. *Op. Cit.*, 58.

²⁶ In addition to Jones' concern about the property tax issue, he had his beliefs about the situation or strategies of action. Decisions regarding behavior usually integrate both beliefs about the object (public officials) and the situation or proposed act. See Milton Rokeach, *Beliefs, Attitudes and Values* (San Francisco: Jossey-Bass, 1968), 143, and Martin Fishbein, "Attitudes and the Prediction of Behavior," in Martin Fishbein (ed.), *Reading in Attitude Theory and Measurement* (New York: John Wiley and Sons, 1967), 477-492.

²⁷ In a similar vein, the fact that blacks score lower on social and political trust scales may have less to do with deep psychological

differences they bring into their daily lives than the fact that they live in areas with high crime rates and intensive police surveillance. The combination of this awareness of possible attack by criminals, and stop-and-search by police because of the color of their skins, will undoubtedly influence their beliefs and affective feelings toward criminals and the police; all of which contributes to their lower social trust. Of course in less threatening environments they might be more trustful. See Paul Abramson, *op. cit.*, Chapters 6-7.

[28] At a more macro level, contradictory or inconsistent results from studies of the influence of family, school and teacher on political attitudes have been related to broad environmental factors such as changing population characteristics which surround and condition the political learning process. These studies do not, however, follow the *same people* within a broad environmental category through different discrete situations to see if their attitudes and behavior are stable, and not reactive to micro forms of environmental stimulus. See, for example, Gunnel Gustafsson, "Environmental Influence on Political Learning," in Richard Niemi (ed.), *The Politics of Future Citizens* (San Francisco: Jossey Bass, 1974), 199-266.

[29] Nie, Powell and Prewitt, *op. cit.*

Chapter 2

SOCIALIZATION AGENTS AND PSYCHODYNAMIC ASSUMPTIONS*

INTRODUCTION

The "primacy" of early learning is a common hypothesis in socialization research.[1] Earlier research normally emphasized some aspect of family socialization. This focus was usually based on the assumed importance of affective ties between parent and child in shaping later political behavior.[2] According to these researchers, one's sense of efficacy is developed with one's parents and it is maintained relatively unchanged throughout the life cycle. In adulthood it influences political behavior.[3]

Contemporary literature has taken a closer and more critical look at the political role of the family and the impact of early learning. Jennings and Niemi found that direct transmission of political values from parents to child was relatively weak.[4] Tedin later demonstrated conditions which strengthened this transmission.[5] Langton found moderate to weak relations between the power structure in the family of origin and adolescents' sense of political efficacy.[6] Clearly, part of the problem in assessing the influence of a socialization agency is to distinguish between the indirect effect of the internal environment (such as the power structure of the family or the class climate of the peer group) and the direct transmission of opinions from parents or peers to their children or friends. In this and the following chapter we shall look at the indirect influence of the participatory culture of the family, school and work group.

As research turned from the family to other socialization agents

---

*Occasional parts of this chapter are drawn from an article by Kenneth P. Langton and David A. Karns, "Political Socialization and National Development: Some Hypotheses and Data," *Western Political Quarterly* 27 (June, 1974), 217-238.

it became apparent that peer groups, school environments, curriculum, teachers, memberships in adult organizations and so on, each contributed in a greater or lesser degree to the formation of political attitudes.[7] If other agents are part of the political socialization process, how does this affect psychodynamic assumptions about the primacy of the family? Is the school or adult work group changing attitudes learned in the family or inculcating new political values? Do adolescent peer groups have more influence on political efficacy than the family of origin?

Most research has focused on single agents. Comparatively few scholars have examined in a single analysis the relative contribution of these experiences. Jennings and Niemi sampled high school seniors in the United States and discovered that their political opinions were somewhat more aligned with those of their parents than with the opinions of their teachers or peers.[8] Langton and Karns found that the political attitudes of Jamaican adolescents were more closely associated with their families than their peer groups or schools.[9] Almond and Verba collected data on different socialization agents in five nations. They examined the relationship between participation in decision-making in family, school and job, and the individual's sense of subjective competence. After analyzing separate contingency tables for each agency, they concluded that the job was the most influential, followed in order by the school and family.[10] It is possible that if they had used some form of multivariant analysis their conclusions might have been different. Their data is rich and extensive, however, and the questions they and the other scholars have raised about the relative influence of the socialization agencies have important implications for our analysis. Should we find that the later agents play as important a role as the family, this would gravitate against the primacy assumptions of the psychodynamic model, at least in the case of political efficacy. Analysis of cross-national data from countries at different levels of development would also make it possible to see if the impact of a socialization agent varies in some systematic fashion with changes in the level of economic and social development of a society. Should this be the case, it would suggest that there is nothing immutable about the importance of early learning for politics.

There are studies which do not focus directly on socialization agencies yet suggest the continuous nature of socialization over the life cycle. For example, Searing, Wright, and Rabinowitz demonstrate that political efficacy is not stable over time for adult populations in the United States. Using cohort analysis they show that between 1952 and 1968 the mean efficacy scores changed on the average of nine percent every four years.[11] They felt these changes were related to undefined period or environmental effects rather than to aging.[12]

In an interesting historical analysis of change in the American electorate, Converse postulates that a "pecking-order" model which imbeds political efficacy in individual traits (and early learning) would predict constant levels of efficacy over time. On the other hand, if an "education-driven" model were operating between 1952 and 1968, political efficacy should increase on the order of five to six percent. This would be commensurate with the aggregate increase in national education. The data did not permit a direct test of these models but Converse comes down on the side of "education-driven" efficacy, given the well-known correlations between levels of education and political efficacy. He points out, however, that efficacy actually declined between 1960 and 1968, while aggregate levels of education increased. Here he draws our attention to "situational setbacks" such as political assassination, Lyndon Johnson's escalation of the Vietnam War, race and campus riots, and widespread resentment concerning forced desegregation that may have contributed to the growing disillusionment.[13]

More recently Jennings and Niemi found significant change in "internal political efficacy" in a two-wave panel study of two biologically linked generations in the United States. The tau-beta correlations between the efficacy scores of high school seniors in 1965 and 1973 was .28; it was .39 for the parents. Although 47 and 69% of the students and parents who were low in efficacy in 1965 were low in 1973, only 38% maintained their high efficacy across this time span.[14]

In Chapters 2 and 3 we shall examine the following:

(1) Possible life cycle changes in political efficacy associated with participation in decisions in one's family of origin in contrast to agencies placed later in the life cycle such as the school and job.

(2) How the influence of these agents varies across different cultures.

(3) How these cross cultural differences might be explained by changes in national levels of socioeconomic development.

(4) What implications points 1 and 3 have for the psychodynamic model.

SOCIALIZATION AGENTS AND NATIONAL DEVELOPMENT

The role of a socialization agent is partially a function of the political and cultural milieu in which it operates. American families contributed significantly to the learning of partisan attachments while the French family was less important in this respect.[15] The formal school environment is not impressive in the development and change of political orientations in the United States, yet scholars stress the part that formal curriculum may play in less industrialized countries.[16]

Does the impact of a socialization agent vary in some systematic manner with changes in the socioeconomic development of that country? To examine this question we shall first set forth a hypothetical model of the linkage between socialization and national socioeconomic development. Then we shall examine national socioeconomic and socialization characteristics to see their "fit" with the model. Within a nation the main unit of analysis will be the individual. Across nations the unit of analysis is a national pattern based on an aggregation of within-nation characteristics.

There are at least two obvious ways in which one can empirically relate socialization to the larger questions of system change. First, there are personality types that have been linked conceptually to socioeconomic and political development. For example, McClelland's achieving personality, Hagen's innovator or Inkeles' modern man provides a point of take-off.[17]

The merging of socioeconomic change and socialization can also be analyzed by first focusing on variations in levels of socioeconomic (or political) development. One must examine the relation between changes in levels of development and the characteristics of different social institutions and their capacity to perform political socialization roles. The output of these socialization agencies, then, closes the socialization-development circle by contributing to the static (or changing) nature of the political and social culture in the respective societies.

Pursuing the second approach, we offer a hypothetical model of how the relative contribution of the family, school and job varies with socioeconomic change in a society. Starting with the family, its influence changes as societies move from pre-industrial to post-industrial levels of development (Figure 2.1).[18] During the pre-industrial phase, the family unit begins to distinguish itself from the lineage group and take its short-extended or nuclear form. Institutionally separate schooling is nonexistent, or, if it does exist, it is only at the primary level which is less culturally distinct from the family than secondary education.[19] Employment is also pre-modern since modern conceptions of work relations, participation, and so on, have not yet penetrated the culture. Under these conditions, the impact of the family is relatively greater than that of the job or school.

FIGURE 2.1. INFLUENCE OF THE FAMILY AND SOCIOECONOMIC DEVELOPMENT

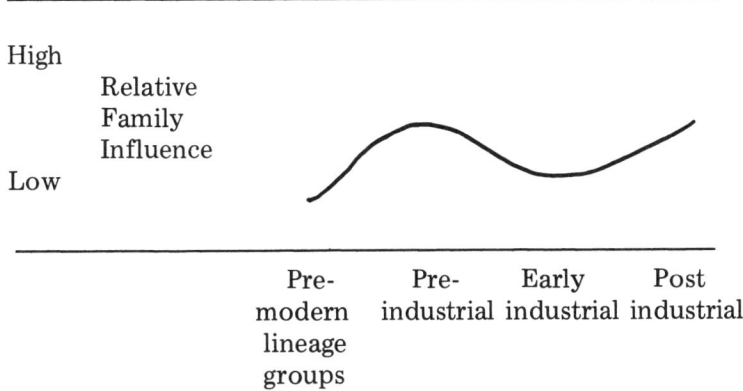

As the country continues to develop socially and economically, a number of important changes occur. First, educational opportunities expand. This is particularly important at the secondary level. In many countries the child must leave home to attend secondary school; thus begins the weakening of family bonds. Edith Clarke provides a moving account of the conscious breaking of family ties among secondary school students in a less industrialized nation.[20] In the school the student is introduced to new norms, aspirations and symbols which increasingly distinguish the culture of the school from that of the family. Formal education begins to compete with the earlier dominance of the family. Second, industrialization means opportunities for modern employment and the penetration of society by new norms regarding work relations and participation. Under these conditions the job as well as the school now compete more effectively with the socialization domain of the family.

In later stages of industrialization, mass communication exposes everyone to an increasingly universal culture. Broadened educational opportunities expand the ranks of the educated, which now include new generations of educated parents as well as their student children. The "modern" norms and modes of conduct that were once the exclusive property of the school in earlier stages of development are increasingly duplicated in the family, where the child has undergone several years of informal political socialization with his more sophisticated parents before he ever reaches secondary school. Thus the school becomes increasingly redundant.[21] Not only is there a repetition of previous cues but also the duplication of cues from other sources, particularly the mass media, peer groups and formal organizations. In short, later stages of socioeconomic development are characterized by the diminished role of the school, while family reaches greater parity with the job in the political socialization process.

VARIABLES AND MEASUREMENTS

A test of these hypotheses requires individual data across nations at different levels of development. In addition, *common* data from different socialization agents as well as from *several facets* of the same agent are necessary. Such data are not available. For the present, however, a partial testing of hypotheses can be carried out with the survey data collected by Gabriel Almond and Sidney Verba. Their study covered five nations: Mexico, United States, Germany, Italy and the United Kingdom.[22] There was one common measurement made across the family, school and job in this study; the respondent's perceptions of the authority patterns in the three agents. Each respondent's political confidence, or "efficacy," was also determined. Thus the hypothesis is (as was Almond and Verba's) that an individual who perceives himself participating in decisions or somehow exerting influence within the authority structure of the family, school and work group, is more likely to generalize this efficacious role to the political arena.[23] That is, he is likely to have a higher level of political efficacy. This could be the result of the early learning of a basic psychological disposition which is generalized to politics in adulthood. Or it could be the result of *stimulus and response generalization*. What one learns in the family may become the basis for future learning in the secondary school or job. The latter emphasizes the cognitive development of the individual as he passes through different settings in the life cycle. There is no assumption that the family of origin will be more influential, for example, than the job. To affect adult participation, past experience in the family must be remembered and judged as being sufficiently similar to characteristics of the present situation. One's confidence that he can have an impact on political authorities in the current situation is affected accordingly. Of course, both processes assume a great many "ifs." Some, but not all, of these will be examined later.

SCALING AND METHOD OF ANALYSIS

Three Guttman scales were constructed which measured the respondent's perceived freedom to participate in and influence the

Socialization Agents and Psychodynamic Assumptions

authority structure of the family, school and work group.[24] Six items which expressed the respondent's sense of confidence in influencing local and national political affairs formed an acceptable Guttman-type efficacy scale in each country.[25]

In constructing the scales we encountered several of the same problems as did other analysts who used the Almond and Verba five-nation data.[26] After consideration, we chose to use Guttman scalogram analysis rather than factor analysis. We believe that each variable taps a single, cumulative dimension. Empirically, the coefficients of reproducibility for each of the five scales in each of the five nations exceeded 0.920. Conceptually, we did not find reasonable response patterns to the questions composing any of the scales which would suggest that the items are not cumulative.[27]

In order to estimate within a single model the relative contribution of family, school and job to the development of political efficacy, we have adopted an analytical technique described by Coleman in his *Introduction to Mathematical Sociology*.[28] The result of this analysis is a set of "causal coefficients" which summarize the influence of each level of the independent variable (socialization agent) as it affects each level of the dependent variable (political efficacy). This statistical technique was selected because we found in the analysis reported in Chapter 3 that many of the relations between the socialization agents and adult political confidence were not linear. Because this finding is of substantive and theoretical importance in the analysis of the psychodynamic model,* we adapted Coleman's technique for a trichotomous dependent variable (low, medium, high political efficacy) to assess the influence of the family, school and work group.

---

*The significance of non-linear relations will be discussed in Chapter 3.

FOOTNOTES AND REFERENCES

[1] For a discussion of the "Primacy Principle" see Donald Searing, Gerald Wright and George Rabinowitz, "The Primacy Principle: Attitude Change and Political Socialization." Mimeo, no date.

[2] For an excellent review of much of the earlier literature and research in political socialization see Jack Dennis, "Recent Research on Political Socialization: A Bibliography of Published, Forthcoming, and Unpublished Works, Theses, and Dissertations, and a Survey of Projects in Progress." Prepared for the Theory and Research Working Committee on Political Socialization of the Council on Civic Education, Lincoln Filene Center for Citizenship and Public Affairs, Tufts University, Medford, Massachusetts, 1967; and John J. Patrick, "Political Socialization of American Youth: A Review of Research with Implications for Secondary School Social Studies," High School Curriculum Center in Government, Indiana University, Bloomington, Indiana, March, 1967.

[3] A correlary of this pychodynamic orientation is the assumption that efficacy is formed during primary school years, since by the eighth grade the mean efficacy of students has been found in some studies to be similar to that of their teachers. Little happens until retirement age, when efficacy appears to decline. If political efficacy does change in late adolescence or the adult years, it will be restricted to periods of grave governmental crises or social upheaval. See Robert Hess and Judith Torney, *The Development of Political Attitudes in Children* (Chicago: Aldine, 1967), Robert Lane, *op. cit.*, 151, and David Easton and Jack Dennis, *Children in the Political System* (New York: McGraw Hill, 1969), 139, 287-313). Also see Arthur Miller, Thad Brown and Alden Raine, "Social Conflict and Political Estrangement," paper delivered at the annual meeting of the Midwest Political Science Association, Chicago, Illinois, May, 1973.

[4] M. Kent Jennings and Richard Niemi, "The Transmission of Political Values from Parents to Child," *American Political Science Review* 62 (March, 1968), 169-184.

[5] Kent L. Tedin, "The Influence of Parents on the Political Attitudes of Adolescents," *American Political Science Review* 68 (December, 1974), 1579-1592.

[6] Kenneth P. Langton, *Political Socialization* (New York: Oxford University Press, 1969), Chap. 2.

[7] For the influence of the class climate of peer groups and schools see Kenneth P. Langton, "Peer Groups and Schools and the Political Socialization Process," *American Political Science Review* 61 (September, 1967), 751-758. M. Kent Jennings and Richard Niemi exam-

ine the direct transmission from teachers and peers in *The Political Character of Adolescence: The Influence of Families and Schools* (Princeton: Princeton University Press, 1974). The impact of organization membership upon political participation is reported by Norman H. Nie, G. Bingham Powell, Jr., and Kenneth Prewitt, "Social Structure and Political Participation: Development Relationships," *American Political Science Review* 63 (June, 1969), 361-378, and 63 (September, 1969), 808-832. The relationship between the high school civics curriculum and student opinions are in Kenneth P. Langton and M. Kent Jennings, "Political Socialization and the High School Civics Curriculum in the United States," *American Political Science Review* 62 (September, 1968), 852-867.

[8] Jennings and Niemi, *The Political Character of Adolescence, Ibid.*

[9] Langton, *Political Socialization, op. cit.*, Chap. 6.

[10] Subjective competence is an attitudinal scale conceptually akin to the political efficacy dimension. Gabriel Almond and Sidney Verba, *The Civic Culture* (Princeton: Princeton University Press, 1963), 371.

[11] Searing, Wright and Rabinowitz, *op. cit.*, 93.

[12] *Ibid.*, 107.

[13] Philip E. Converse, "Change in the American Electorate" mimeo, no date, 92-105.

[14] M. Kent Jennings and Richard G. Niemi, "The Persistence of Political Orientations: An Over-time Analysis of Two Generations," *British Journal of Political Science* 8 (July, 1978), 343-344.

[15] Philip E. Converse and Georges Dupuex, "Politicization of the Electorate in France and the United States," *Public Opinion Quarterly*, 26 (1962), 1-23.

[16] Langton and Jennings, *op. cit.*, 852-867: John Vaizey, "Economics of Education," *International Social Science Journal* 14 (1962), 627; Frederick Harbison and Charles A. Myers, *Education, Manpower, and Economic Growth* (New York: McGraw-Hill, 1964); Dwaine Marvick, "African University Students: A Presumptive Elite," in James S. Coleman (ed.), *Education and Political Development* (Princeton, Princeton University Press, 1965), 463-497; Leonard M. Thompson, *Politics in the Republic of South Africa* (Boston: Little, Brown, 1966); Richard R. Fagen, Cuba: *The Political Content of Adult Education* (Stanford: The Hoover Institution of War and Peace, 1964); and Kenneth Prewitt (ed.), *Education and Political Values: Essays about East Africa* (Nairobi: East African Publishing House, 1969).

[17] David McClelland, *The Achieving Society* (New York: Van

Nostrand, 1961); E. Hagen, *On the Theory of Social Change* (Homewood, Illinois: The Dorsey Press, 1962); and Alex Inkeles, "Making Men Modern," *American Journal of Sociology* 75 (September, 1969), 208-225.

[18] For a provocative social history of family life from medieval to modern times see Philippe Aries, *Centuries of Childhood* (New York: Knopf, 1962). Also, see Daniel R. Miller and Guy E. Swanson, *The Changing American Parent* (New York: Wiley, 1958).

[19] Syed Nurulla and J. P. Nalik, *A History of Education in India* (Bombay: Macmillan, 1951); George Harley, "Notes on the Poro in Liberia," *Peabody Museum Papers*, Vol. 19, No. 2 (1941); Frank Bonilla, "Brazil" in James S. Coleman (ed.), *Education and Political Development* (Princeton: Princeton University Press, 1965), 199; and Malcolm H. Kerr's discussion of "elementary" education in Egypt *op. cit.*, 174-175; Robert LeVine, "Political Socialization and Cultural Change," in Clifford Geerts (ed.), *Old Societies and New States* (New York: Free Press, 1963), 282; Helen Kitchen (ed.), *The Educated African* (New York: Praeger, 1962), 145-159; Alexander T. Edelman, *Latin American Politics and Government* (Homewood, Illinois: Dorsey, 1965), 120-124; and UNESCO, *World Survey of Education, II: Primary Education* (Paris, 1958).

[20] Edith Clarke, *My Mother Who Fathered Me* (London: Allen and Unwin, 1957); Madeline Kerr, *Personality and Conflict in Jamaica* (Liverpool: University Press, 1952); George F. Kneller, *The Education of the Mexican Nation* (New York: Columbia University Press, 1951).

[21] For an examination of the possible effect of information redundancy on school socialization in the United States, see Langton and Jennings, "Political Socialization and the High School Civics Curriculum in the United States," *op. cit.*

[22] *The Civic Culture, op. cit.* For sampling procedures and survey methods employed, see Chapter 2 and Appendices A and B in *The Civic Culture*. There are some data and sampling problems in the five nation study, such as the "urban" nature of the Mexican sample and the fact that certain groups are not proportionately represented in the Italian sample. We are sensitive to these problems and do introduce controls for education level. As for the urban bias in Mexico, few people who are knowledgeable of Latin American culture would consider a town of 10,000 as urban by United States standards. In any case, any "urban bias" in the Mexican sample will only tend to strengthen our conclusions as will be clear in the analysis.

The Civic Culture is a classic contribution to the study and literature of comparative politics. We would like to add our acknowledgement and express appreciation to Professors Almond and Verba for making available to the discipline a body of data that has had a seminal effect on the development and preliminary testing of many a hypothesis.

[23] Leroy S. Burwen and Donald T. Campbell, "The Generality of Attitudes toward Authority and Non-authority Figures," *Journal of Abnormal and Social Psychology*, 54 (1957), 24-31.

[24] *Participation in Family Scale*
Items:
1. As you were growing up, let's say when you were around 16, how much influence do you remember having in family decisions affecting yourself—did you have much influence, some, or none at all?
2. At around the same time, if a decision were made that you didn't like, did you feel free to complain, did you feel a little uneasy about complaining, or was it better not to complain?
3. If you complained, did it make any difference in your parents' decision—did it make a lot of difference, some, or none?

Participation in School
Items:
1. In some schools the children are encouraged to discuss and debate political and social issues and to make up their own minds. How was it in your school—how much chance did the children have to express their opinions—a lot, some, or none at all?
2. If you felt you had been treated unfairly in some way or disagreed with something the teacher had said, did you feel free to talk with the teacher about it, did you feel a bit uneasy about talking to the teacher, or was it better not to talk to the teacher?
3. Would it have made any difference—a lot, some, or none?

Participation in the Job
Items:
1. We'd like to find out how decisions are made on your job. When decisions are made affecting your own work, do those in authority over you ever consult you about them—do they usually consult you, do they sometimes consult you, do they rarely consult you, or are you never consulted?
2. If a decision were made affecting your own work that you disagreed with strongly, what would you do—would you feel free to complain, would you feel uneasy about complaining, or is it better to accept the decision and not complain?
3. If you did complain, would it do any good?

[25] Almond and Verba devised a five-item subjective competence scale which they felt measured the "extent to which (respondents) *believe* themselves competent in their relations with government"

[emphasis ours]. However, one of the five items seems to be informational while another stresses participation. This poses a dimensionality problem.

The efficacy scale used in Chapters 2 and 3 differs from the subjective competence measure on at least two counts. First, we only used the three original items which stress a subjective perception or belief in personal influence. Adding the participation item would not only raise the dimensionality question but, equally important, it would increase artificially the correlation between measures of efficacy and political participaton. Second, the subjective competence measure stressed only local competence while our six point measure includes, in addition, three items reflecting perceptions of efficacy at the national level.

[26] Nie, Powell, and Prewitt, *op. cit.*

[27] If we accept the position that a Guttman or cumulative model is more applicable than a point preference model, the analyst should use either scalogram analysis or a factor analysis of a matrix of tetrachoric correlation coefficients. Factor analysis of a matrix containing product moment correlations which have been generated by data based on the Guttman model will not necessarily reproduce the spatial locations of variables correctly. Consequently we chose to use scalogram analysis. We feel that the item rotation which developed in some cases contained valuable information which would be omitted in a factor analysis. In other words, if questions 27 and 29 were in that order in the scalogram analysis for Germany, but 29 and 27 for Italy, this datum would offer insight into national differences. To guarantee comparability cross-nationally, we performed separate scalogram analysis on each sample rather than assuming a single scale order was applicable to all five nations.

[28] James S. Coleman, *Introduction to Mathematical Sociology* (Glencoe: Free Press, 1964), Chap. 4. For a discussion of our application of this technique see Kenneth P. Langton and David A. Karns, "Political Socialization and National Development: Some Hypotheses and Data," *Western Political Quarterly* 27 (June, 1974), 217-238; and "The Relative Influence of the Family, Peer Group, and School in the Development of Political Efficacy," the *Western Political Quarterly* 22 (December, 1969), 818, 823-826.

Chapter 3

FAMILY, SCHOOL, JOB AND POLITICAL EFFICACY

(Co-Authored by David A. Karns*)

INTRODUCTION

What effect does participation in the family, school and work group have on an adult's sense of political efficacy? Do these relationships change as one moves from less to more industrialized countries? What are the implications of these findings for the psychodynamic linkage between early participation in the family and school and an adult's feeling of political confidence?

Before turning to the analysis we should caution the reader on a few points. The respondents in the five national surveys are asked about power arrangements in their family of origin, school, and job. The question here is whose perception of the freedom to participate in decisions should be used? The view of the respondent, for example, may differ significantly from those of his parents and siblings. Their perceptions, in turn, may differ from those of an "independent observer" of the family scene.[1] As interesting or troublesome as this may seem methodologically, the focus here is on the agential environment as the respondent sees it.

When we refer in the following analysis to the "influence" of the family, the reference is to the relation between the perception of adults about their past participation in a socialization agency and

---

*Parts of this chapter are based on an extension and revision by Kenneth P. Langton of an article by Kenneth P. Langton and David A. Karns, "Political Socialization and National Development: Some Hypotheses and Data," *Western Political Quarterly* 27 (June, 1974), 217-238. Citations of this chapter should list authors in this order: Kenneth P. Langton and David A. Karns.

their current political confidence. From a psychodynamic perspective, adult efficacy reflects the primacy of these early paths of influence. There is a potential methodological problem with this assumption, however. When adults are asked to recall the environment of their parents' family they may not be able to remember. Forgetting may be greater among the older respondents when they reflect on their early family milieu. The only accurate test of this confounding problem involves a panel study controlling for the impact of agents outside the family. The data in the five-nation study are cross-sectional, not longitudinal. It is possible, however, to draw some inferences about the effects of simple forgetting with the passage of time. Experimental psychological research on attitude change shows that the rate of forgetting the character of a persuasive communication diminishes over time. As Arthur Cohen says, "... we forget most rapidly immediately after learning, and in successive equal time intervals we forget proportionately less...."[2] One might expect, by inference, that the principal distortion of perceptions occurs within a relatively short period after leaving the environment of the home or school. To test this hypothesis, we broke the respective national samples into separate age cohorts.[3] The largest shift in remembrance occurs among the youngest age group, shortly after direct family socialization experience has normally ceased. Thus the findings reflect more closely the literature in experimental psychology than the stereotypic image of aging and increased memory loss. This analysis is only suggestive. It does imply, however, that forgetting as measurement error is much more complicated than ordinarily assumed and that its form may be quite different at various points in the life cycle.

The implications of memory loss are quite different if one turns from psychodynamic assumptions to cognitive processes. In the former, memory loss is a methodological problem. It increases the difficulty of measuring accurately the power structure of the family of origin via the perceptions of the adult respondent. If memory loss is severe it could attenuate the magnitude of the relations we shall report later in the chapter.* For the cognitive psychologist trying to explain the decision of adults to participate in politics, the *relevance* of early experiences in the family, as well as our inclination to forget them, are important data. It may be that we do remember generally whether we were allowed to participate in family decisions. Yet we find the characteristic of those situations to be

---

*As we shall see, many of the relations between socialization agents and the political efficacy of the adult respondents are quite strong.

quite different from current contexts in which we are trying to decide whether to campaign, demonstrate or petition. No matter how confident we felt about working things out with our parents, it may be difficult to generalize from those early experiences to the present situation with its different characteristics.

Certainly as we search past experiences for decision guides to a current situation, we may simply forget what happened to us in the family and school. Most of the respondents, however, did report their participation experiences in the family, school and job.* Thus in terms of the cognitive process involved, the *relevance* of these past experiences may be the most important datum in predicting the decision of adults to participate in politics.

ANALYSIS

In the course of the analysis we found that the relations between participating in the socialization agents and the respondents' political efficacy were not linear. Non-linear relations have received little attention in socialization research. As they may prove fundamental to our eventual understanding of the socialization process and hold important implications for our examination of the psychodynamic model, we feel the following methodological detour is warranted.

Non-linearity:

The following example should illustrate the substantive importance of non-linear relations. In the United States the correlation between students' participation in family decision-making and their development of a sense of political efficacy might be on the order of .26. On the other hand, encouraging student participation and discussion in school correlates at the .18 level with efficacy. How do we interpret these two correlations? First, family appears to be somewhat more influential than the school but both correlations are relatively low. In fact, correlations of this magnitude are often used as a case *against* significant linkages. Aside from depressed correlation coefficients, what is the significance if the relation between the particular agent and the dependent variable is not linear? Tables 3.1 and 3.2 are hypothetical examples of two truncated relations.

---

*If we adopt a cognitive processing approach, the accuracy of recall is less important than the role these perceptions play as they form a part of our past situational experience which we *consider relevant* to the current decision to participate (GxBxC—F).

A change in school participation is associated with a 20% increase in *medium* efficacy. The school has little effect in moving respondents into the *high* efficacy range. On the other hand, family participation is most effective at the high efficacy level (Table 3.2). It is possible that the broader, less intimate school environment reaches the zenith of its influence at the medium level. Only the face-to-face milieu of such groups as the family or peer group is effective in what may be the more difficult task of moving people from medium to high efficacy. Conversely, the family may be particularly important in inculcating medium efficacy, but reaches its maximum influence at that level; thus it is the responsibility of secondary agencies such as the school and job to move the adolescent, and later the adult, into higher reaches of political confidence. If this were indeed the case, it would argue against the psychodynamic notion that family learning is necessarily the most crucial stage in the development of political efficacy. This would be particularly true if a high sense of efficacy were generally required to spur people into participating in politics.

FAMILY, SCHOOL, JOB AND EFFICACY

Figure 3.1 shows the relation of family, school and work group participation to a sense of political efficacy in the five nations. An arrow in these figures identifies a relation between an agent and efficacy which is greater than zero. The number affixed to each arrow is the dependency (D) coefficient expressed as a percentage.[4] This is not a regression coefficient. The coefficient symbolizes, instead, the percentage of the sample that moves from one efficacy level to another, say from low to medium, due to its exposure to a participatory environment in one of the socialization agencies. This is done holding constant the effect of the other two agencies.*

Relative Effects:

Summing the coefficients for each of the three agents across the five countries shows the face-to-face environment of the job and family to be more strongly associated with a sense of efficacy than

---

*This coefficient is roughly analogous to the result obtained from squaring a correlation coefficient to determine the percent of variance explained. In Great Britain a coefficient of .168 between job participation and medium efficacy equals 16.8% and signifies that exposure to a participatory job environment is independently associated with the placement of 16.8% of the *sample* in the medium efficacy range.[5] Job participation is associated with the placement of 7.6% at the high efficacy level.

TABLE 3.1

Relation Between Participation in School Decision-making and Political Efficacy*

School Participation	Political Efficacy		
	Low	Medium	High
	%	%	%
Low	42	50	8
High	21	70	9

TABLE 3.2

Relation Between Participation in Family Decision-making and Political Efficacy*

Family Participation	Political Efficacy		
	Low	Medium	High
	%	%	%
Low	55	40	5
High	50	25	25

*Hypothetical tables

FIGURE 3.1
RELATIONS BETWEEN FAMILY, SCHOOL AND WORK GROUP PARTICIPATION AND POLITICAL EFFICACY IN FIVE COUNTRIES

UNITED STATES

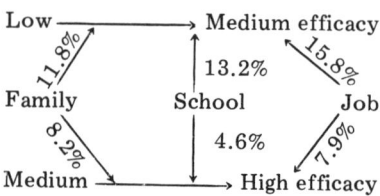

GREAT BRITAIN

GERMANY

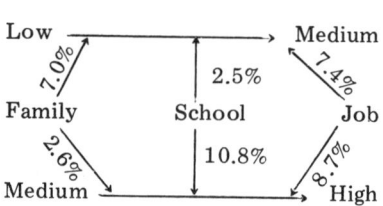

ITALY

MEXICO

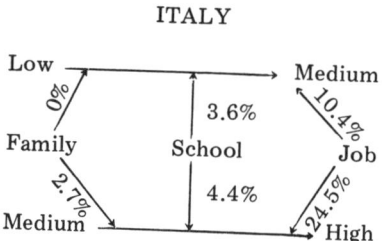
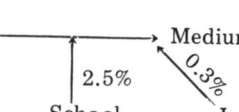

the broader, less intimate milieu of the school. This finding is similar to previous experience with high school students in which the family and peer group were more influential than the wider, less personal milieu of the school in developing a sense of political confidence.[6]

Linear Relations:

The relationships between agents and efficacy in Figure 3.1 are not linear. For example, job does not have equal impact at the medium and high efficacy levels. In Great Britain its major influence is in developing medium (16.8%) rather than high (7.6%) efficacy. Clearly, a mode of analysis based on the assumption of linear relations would have obscured important differences in the data.

Comparing the strength of the relations between the agents and different levels of the dependent variable shows faint patterns across the five nations. Job is slightly more important than family in moving people from low to medium efficacy, followed at some distance by the impact of school.[7] At this level, job participation is marginally more influential in the United States, Great Britain, and Italy, equalled by family influence in Germany, while the family link is stronger in Mexico. The pattern is also uneven at the high efficacy level. The family is somewhat more effective than the job (three of five countries), again followed by the school.

The truncated effect of the socialization agents might be clearer if we controlled for education. It seems intuitively reasonable that the relative influence of job participation will decline as education increases. The job must then compete with other sources such as the media which are increasingly available to the more educated. Moreover, the quality of family life, information levels, transmission of political cues, and length of adolescence in the educated family distinguishes it from families with less educated parents. The political environment of these families may have made past participation in them more relevant to present political situations in which adults find themselves.* On the other hand, children from these families also have been bombarded by a broad array of stimulants from outside the family which is likely to have moved them into at least the medium efficacy level.[8] Therefore, among the most educated, the link between family and efficacy may be stronger in the high efficacy range.

The data show that among the most educated strata in the four

---

*This assumes, of course, a cognitive rather than a psychodynamic process.

more developed countries, the relation between family and high efficacy is almost twice as strong as that of either the job or school. The three agents have equal effect at the medium efficacy level. The job is more important among those with only a primary school education. Moreover, job exerts a strong effect at both the medium and high efficacy levels among the less educated. To summarize, the family link is strongest among the educated, since it dominates the movement from medium to high efficacy. The job is most effective among the least educated, where its impact is felt both in the medium and high efficacy range.

These findings suggest the important formative role of the job late in the life cycle. This conclusion questions the assumption that political efficacy is learned early. While efficacy clearly responds to family environment,* job moves adults with only primary school education into the medium efficacy level. Other data also cast doubt on the assumption that efficacy is relatively stable across the life cycle. When less educated workers encounter participatory job environments, it moves significant numbers of them who earlier in life had acquired a medium sense of efficacy into the high range.

National Development and Socialization:

On the most commonly used indicators of economic and social development in the mid-1960's—percent of labor force in service occupations, per capita gross national product, media participation— Mexico[9] was the least developed, United States and Great Britain the most developed, and Germany[10] and Italy usually somewhere in between (Table 3.3).

Earlier we hypothesized that the links between socialization agents and the objects of socialization are likely to vary with the level of socioeconomic development. To briefly recapitulate, during the pre-industrial phase the family begins to distinguish itself from the lineage group and take a short-extended or nuclear form. Schooling outside of the family is not likely to exist or to operate only at the primary level which is not culturally distinct from the family. The work environment is pre-modern; new work norms have not penetrated or exist only at low intensity levels. At this stage in development the family dominates the socialization process.

---

*Whether this is the result of a psychodynamic or cognitive process we shall try to clarify later.

TABLE 3.3

Ranking of Five Countries By Measures of Economic and Social Development

Country	Real GNP Per Head 1961 ($USA)[a]	% Labor Force in Service Occupations 1960[b]	Newsprint Consumption Per Person (kilograms) 1960[b]
U.S.A.	$2790.	42.0%	36.6
Great Britain	1749.	39.8	24.9
Germany	1591.	29.9	9.6
Italy	897.	22.9	5.3
Mexico	415.	21.3	2.9

Sources:

[a] Gross National Product (GNP) per head is an estimate of purchasing power in terms of United States dollars at United States 1961 prices. See P. D. Rosenstein-Rodan, "International Aid for Underdeveloped Countries," *The Review of Economics and Statistics*, 63 (May, 1961).

[b] United Nations, *Compendium of Social Statistics: 1963* (New York: 1963).

As economic and social development continues, culturally distinguishable secondary education expands. Industrialization leads to different forms of employment that penetrate society and intensify participation norms and new work relations. Both the school and job now compete with and displace the earlier dominance of the family. In later stages of development the quality of family life changes as parents become more educated and attentive to politics. The relative influence of the school decreases as the norms and information it imparts become increasingly redundant and the impact of family reaches greater parity with job influence. If the socialization role of these agencies does react to broader societal changes as hypothesized, we have an argument against the psychodynamic notion about the unchanging primacy of particular sets of agents within the socialization process.

To see how these propositions are reflected in the data, we summed the dependency coefficients linking each socialization agent to political efficacy. This was done within each of the three groups of countries which are at different levels of socioeconomic development. In Table 3.4 the numbers in parentheses equal the sum (%) of each agent's influence in both countries. Relative differences in the effect of the three agents *within* developmental levels are important here, not absolute differences across levels. Greater-than symbols indicate substantial differences in effect, while equal-to or greater-than symbols show rough equality.

TABLE 3.4

Relation Between Family, School, and Job Participation and Political Efficacy by Developmental Level

---

Job (48) $\geqslant$ Family (44) > School (24): United States, United Kingdom

Job (51) > School (21) > Family (12): Germany, Italy

Family (23) > School (6) $\geqslant$ Job (2): Mexico

Among the five countries surveyed, Mexico most closely resembles a less-developed country. Here the family dominates the political socialization process, followed at considerable distance by the school and job. In Italy and Germany, two countries in the middle rank of the developmental scale, family primacy is displaced by the enlarged roles of the work group and school. In the United States and Great Britain, the two most developed countries, the influence of the increasingly redundant school predictably declines in relative importance. At the same time, the family re-asserts itself and now rivals the job. The changing patterns of influence do follow the development-socialization model presented earlier.

The Mexican data are closest to the psychodynamic conception of the dominant role of the family in political learning. What will happen as the modern industrial sector expands in Mexico and more children are exposed to secondary education? In 1960, about 12 percent of the school-age population was enrolled in academic secondary schools which introduced the student to the culture most likely to be different from that of the family.[11] If the culture of secondary schools in less developed countries penetrates traditional family influence, this should be born out in the data among the subsample of Mexicans with a secondary education. Looking only at the group that has had some secondary education changes significantly the relation between the three agents and efficacy in Mexico. Participation in secondary school is associated with the placement of 28 percent of the subsample in the medium and high levels of efficacy as compared to 8 percent for the family, and 3 percent for the job. Moreover, the impact of the family is at the medium efficacy level, while the school plays an important role in moving those who developed medium efficacy in the family into the higher reaches of political confidence.

In all countries, except Great Britain, the impact of the job is reduced or low among those with more education. The increased social contacts, varied and competing sources of information, and generally wider horizons of the more educated combine to reduce the influence of the job. On the other hand, those in the developed countries with only primary education are less likely to have learned participatory skills in the family. Among this group, the job, if it inculcates modern norms related to participation and the sense of political confidence, should have greater influence. There is support for this proposition in the United States, Germany, and Italy since the association between work group participation and political efficacy is larger at the primary level (Table 3.5).

TABLE 3.5

D Coefficient (%) Between Job Participation and Political Efficacy, by Education

	Secondary or More	Primary or less
United States	08.8%	19.0%
Great Britain	31.0	23.5
Germany	00.0	16.3
Italy	06.4	37.4

Only in Great Britain does work environment have a significant influence on political efficacy both among those with high and low education. Organized labor in Great Britain has played an important role in intensifying the employee's sense of job participation and its translation into political confidence, both among the lower and middle classes. For example, British unskilled, skilled, and white collar workers all distinguish themselves from their counterparts in the other nations by their greater sense of freedom to protest job decisions that are not in their interest.

If one adopts a purely psychodynamic approach it is difficult to explain the British case. From a cognitive point of view, however, this is a classic example of experience in a "non-political" environment becoming the past situational participation *most* relevant to current beliefs about one's political effectiveness. Work environments in Britain have long been politicized. For many people they represent their only past political participation. It is no wonder then that workers find it easier to generalize from these experiences to current feelings about political effectiveness.

IMPLICATIONS OF FINDINGS FOR PSYCHODYNAMIC ASSUMPTIONS

Participation in family decision-making as a child is associated with the respondent's sense of political efficacy. It is not known whether this is the result of the early formation of a stable personality disposition (G→A) or a cognitive process in which past situations in the family are seen as similar to current contexts and therefore instructive to one's sense of situational efficacy (GxB→C). While we cannot test this question directly, the data in this and following chapters point away from psychodynamic explanations and more in the direction of continuous social learning.

First, the notion that family is the prime socialization source for political confidence across most societies is weakened when the socialization role of the family changes as countries undergo socioeconomic transformation. Moreover, political efficacy is not always early learned. Among the educated subsample in Mexico, it is the secondary school, not earlier family experience, that accounts for most movement into the medium and high efficacy range. Nor do the data support the contention that political efficacy is stable across the life cycle. Other studies have noted the mean changes in efficacy levels between 1952 and 1968 in the United States. We found the milieu of the work organization plays an important formative role among less educated workers. It takes those who had acquired a low or medium sense of efficacy earlier in life and moves them into the higher reaches of political confidence.

The preceding analysis argues neither for the primacy of the family nor for the stability of efficacy across the life cycle. It would now be useful to move from broad time periods *qua* environment to a finer probing of those real life situations which influence an adult's sense of political efficacy.

Scholars generally do hold constant environmental categories such as education or occupation to see if people from dissimilar backgrounds have different levels of political efficacy. Our conceptual assumptions, however, do not lead us to follow the *same people* within an environmental category or time period through different sociopolitical contexts to see if these individual psychological differences are indeed stable, and not reactive to situational stimuli. If the political confidence of a person reacts not only to changing conditions across the life cycle or long time periods, but also to changes in situations during more restricted periods in adulthood, this would further limit the psychodynamic process. We examine this possibility in Chapter 5. Chapter 6 investigates the final link in the psychodynamic model; the ability of a general sense of political efficacy to predict participation decisions (A→F).

Psychodynamic linkages formed only part of the network of predictors discussed in Chapter 1. In the next chapter we will operationalize a design for incorporating personality, situations and the other predictors in Figure 1.1 into a cognitive-interaction framework.

FOOTNOTES AND REFERENCES

[1] Robert Hess and Judith Torney, "The Child's Idealization of Authority," unpublished manuscript, 1962; and Richard Niemi, "A Methodological Study of Political Socialization in the Family," Ph.D. Dissertation, University of Michigan, Department of Political Science, 1967.

[2] Arthur R. Cohen, *Attitude Change and Social Influence* (New York: Basic Books, 1964), 13. Also see N. H. Anderson and A. A. Barrios, "Primacy Effects in Personality Impression Formation," *Journal of Abnormal and Social Psychology* 69 (1961), 35-40; and Norman Miller and Donald T. Campbell, "Recency and Primacy in persuasion as a Function of the Timing of Speeches and Measurements," *Journal of Abnormal and Social Psychology* 59 (1959), 1-9.

³ Representing the distortion effects as a first order Markov chain, we used the cohort perceptions of family and school participation quasi-longitudinally. The simplex solution for linear programming problems offered a technique for estimating the entries in the Markov transformation matrices while constraining the entries to the interval between 0 and 1. See William J. Baumol, *Economic Theory and Operations Analysis*, 2nd edition (Englewood Cliffs: Prentice-Hall, 1965), Chap. 5.

⁴ The percentages in subsequent tables and figures actually represent the product of multiplying the D coefficient by 100.

⁵ This is analogous, in a multivariate sense, with a quasi-experimental procedure of grouping a population on different states of an independent variable and comparing the difference in conditional probabilities of achieving given states of a dependent variable. As stated above, the coefficient of .168 in Great Britain indicates that exposure to job participation is related to the movement of 16.8% of the *sample* into the medium efficacy range. However, only 58% of the sample reached the medium level on the efficacy scale. Therefore, the coefficient of 16.8 actually accounts for the placement of 29% of those *found* at the *medium efficacy level.*

⁶ Kenneth P. Langton and David A. Karns, "The Relative Role of Family, Peer Group and School in the Development of Political Efficacy," *Western Political Quarterly* (December, 1969), 813-826.

⁷ The sum of the D coefficients leading from job, family, and school to medium efficacy for all five countries is .51, .46, and .22, respectively.

⁸ Angus Campbell, Philip Converse, Warren Miller, and Donald Stokes, *The American Voter* (New York: Wiley, 1960).

⁹ The Mexican survey data have a slight urban bias; thus, this subuniverse would register somewhat higher on Table 3.3 than would the national aggregates. (See Chapter 2, footnote 21.)

¹⁰ Although Italy clearly shared characteristics with less developed countries, Germany intuitively seemed closer in the 1960s to the developmental level of the United States and Great Britain. However, the experience of Germany, particularly after World War II, resembled in some respects that of new nations in the early stages of social development. Faced with the problem of creating a new political culture, the country needed to rebuild and change the schools. To the degree that programs to increase student participation in the schools and make the classroom more democratic have been realized ("Burgerverantwortung in der Gemeide," Frankfort am Main: Institut Zur Forderung Offentlicher Angelegenheiten, 1950), the ensuing reduction in school redundancy would be similar in effect to the penetration of early industrial societies by modern secondary educa-

tion. That is, we might expect school participation in Germany to have a strong impact upon political efficacy, particularly at the secondary level.

[11] Document No. 49 presented by the General Secretary of UNESCO to the Conference on Education and Social and Economic Development in Latin America (Santiago, Chile, 1962). Cited in Aldo Solari, "Secondary Education and the Development of Elites," in Seymour Lipset and Aldo Solari (eds.), *Elites in Latin America* (New York: Oxford University Press, 1967), 459.

The UNESCO figure of 12 percent is closely reflected by the 15 percent of the Mexican sample who responded that they had attended a secondary or advanced technical school.

Chapter 4

COGNITIVE PROCESSES AND THE INCLUSION OF SITUATIONS
A QUASI-EXPERIMENTAL APPROACH

The data requirements for examining the possible interaction between situations and psychological dispositions are demanding. For example, voting studies which investigate the influence of context find that people who are cross-pressured by friends and family behave differently from those who are not. These studies do not normally, however, follow the *same* people in and out of cross-pressured situations and examine the effect on political behavior of the interaction between situations and attitudes. Case studies in public administration and organizational behavior are often sensitive to contextual stimuli. Before and after research on the effect of changes in the work environment (lighting, music, etc.) upon the productivity of workers is well known. These designs, however, are not widely applied in political science, nor in public administration, for that matter. The theoretical requirements of such a study necessitate following the same people across a series of situations, cataloguing the variation or constancy of their attitudes or dispositions and observing their behavior in each situation. Then one must determine how much of that behavior is explained by the individuals' attitudes, characteristics of the different situations, and the interaction between attitudes and situations.

To examine the core of Figure 1.1 (see Figure 4.1) and the complexities of the cognitive processing approach outlined in Chapter 1, we must first find individuals who are concerned enough about politics to enter situations in which they could decide to participate. Political interest or centrality of the issue is one of those watersheds which moves some people to act and many more to stay out of public politics.

In addition to political interest, enough people must have participated in similar situations so that there is sufficient variance in prior learning. At time 1 we measure their general political efficacy, as it is generally assumed that it will affect their later decision to participate. At time 2 the situation develops. For example, the subject is approached about joining a petition drive to force local authorities to reconsider their stand on school bussing. He is deciding whether he is concerned enough to act. Political awareness and centrality of the issue are important data points. If the person is concerned, he will try to decide whether his action will influence the authorities in question (situational efficacy).

If feelings of efficacy are generalizable across situations, the measure of general efficacy (T_1) should reflect situational efficacy (T_2). A fair test of this first hypothesis requires that the situational efficacy measure be identical to the general efficacy measure, except that it be directed toward the authorities in the particular context, rather than authorities in general.

In trying to decide whether the petition drive will have an effect on the officials in question, certain stimuli in the situation shape the subject's expectancy about possible outcomes based on what he learned before in similar situations.* He may also have heard from friends who joined a petition drive last year who said that they did not feel it had any effect on these same authorities. In time 2, then, situational efficacy, prior situational participation, and knowledge of the situational experience of others must be measured. We need also to probe other factors such as peer influence, sense of obligation to participate, desire for "kicks," and so on, which may motivate an individual to participate regardless of his sense of situational efficacy. In time 3, we observe whether the subject does participate or not.

Pretest:

In order to have a better grasp of the dynamics of Figure 4.1 in the real world, we began observing six politically active individuals. To enhance the generality of the findings, we only tried to observe those situations which involved influence strategies that were available to most of the adult population, and were frequently employed by

---

*The S may have used other strategies which were successful and his confidence in the past efficacy of these strategies may spill over into this situation. This will be considered in Chapter 6.

Cognitive Processes And The Inclusion of Situations

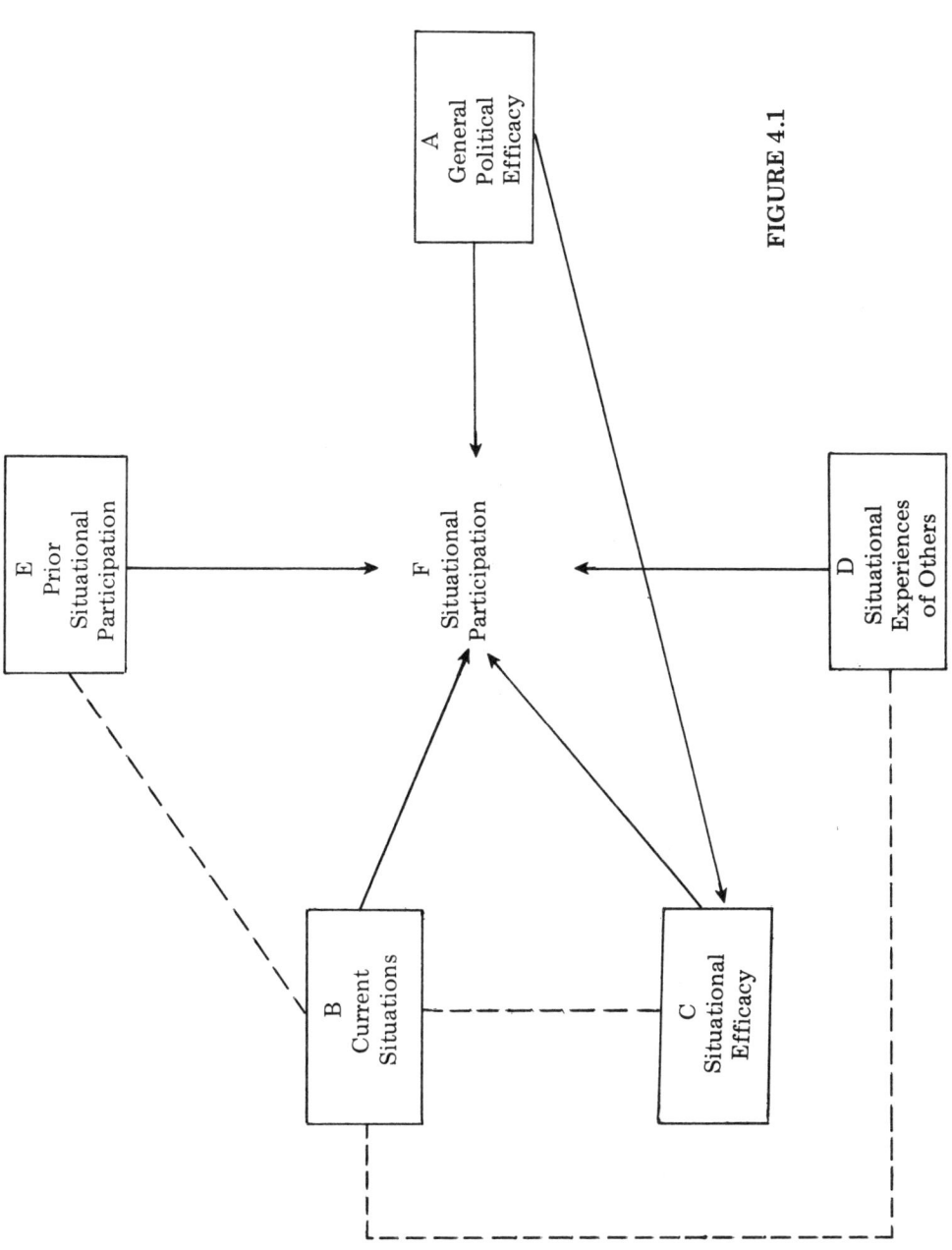

FIGURE 4.1

the attentive public. Bombings and political assassinations were forsaken for the more mundane strategies: voting, letter-writing, petitioning, demonstrating, and campaigning. Of course, reducing the range of situations potentially reduces the amount of variance in participation accounted for by situations.

Following the design requirements suggested above, we first interviewed the six subjects to determine their general political efficacy level. During the next eight months, through participant observation and interviews, we were able to observe sixteen situations involving four different strategies. In each situation an individual weighed the likelihood that a particular strategy would have some influence on political authority. One subject was encountered in four different action situations (picketing, voting, letter-writing, and petitioning). Two subjects were in three strategy situations, and three subjects in two situations.

To summarize briefly the results of the pretest, the political confidence of five of the six subjects changed (within individual) and interchanged (across individuals) as they were observed in different strategy-situations. There also was a relationship between their confidence that a particular strategy would be influential ("If I help picket they [authorities] are going to act") and their tendency to participate, although that relationship was not perfect. In shaping expectations about outcomes, situational stimuli were more likely to cue past personal experiences than what the subjects had heard from others.

During this period we also had occasion to observe the interaction between situations and dispositions as subjects placed themselves mentally in different situations. During a meeting about the Vietnam War one strategist was advocating a petition drive to make the state legislature publicly condemn the war. Another observed that this was a waste of time; the only way to influence a member of the legislature was to make sure you put the right one in office in the first place. "We have to join the elections campaigns," she protested, "that is the only way to make them respond." As the discussion continued each person's sense of confidence—that he or she could influence political authorities—varied as different strategies, levels of government or other characteristics of potential action situations were discussed. At another meeting, a political coalition was discussing which actions would be most effective in influencing U.S. officials and their policy toward a particular Latin American country. Political confidence ebbed and flowed as different strategies were advocated. Attitudes differed across individuals, and verbal expressions of political confidence changed *within individuals* as they weighed the "pros and cons" of alternative strategies and the different characteristics of potential action situations.

Test:

Observing and recording individual behavior and attitudes in a variety of real life situations was not feasible for large groups of people. Because our observations did not suggest major theoretical alterations to Figure 4.1, we decided to adopt a quasi-experimental method, enlarge the sample, and make it more representative of the attentive public.

First, we developed an interview format to try to meet the requirements of Figure 4.1. But pretests suggested that little was gained by interviews over less costly paper-and-pencil questionnaires. Moreover, there was some evidence that interviews introduced unwanted interviewer noise to the test. In November and December, 1972, 530 upper division university students were asked to complete in a classroom setting a paper-and-pencil questionnaire. Ninety-eight percent of the students were older then 18 years and studying in the College of Literature, Science or the Arts at a large midwestern university.*

In the first section of the questionnaire there were six of the standard general efficacy questions commonly used in the literature.[1] Interspersed with these questions were probes about the subject's background, awareness of politics, and interest in some of the popular issues of the day.

In the second section of the questionnaire, the subjects were given written descriptions of a variety of real life situations, in which they faced the possibility of an influence attempt on some distinct political authority. Three levels of authority were analyzed: national, local (city) and university. Level of government was introduced because earlier observations indicated people felt that some governmental authorities were less amenable to influence than others. Pretests also showed that these were the levels of authority in which these adults were most interested and aware.

Within each of the three levels of authority five influence strategies were probed: voting, letter-writing, petitioning, campaigning and demonstrating.** Each strategy-level combination was imbedded in

---

*Characteristics of the student sample will be discussed later.

**During pretests, these were the five strategies the respondents mentioned most often as being available to the general public.

a written description of a realistic event that we found from the pretest to be familiar to most of the population, through either direct or vicarious experience. This made a total of fifteen situations. Besides the strategy-level dimensions, the situations had other characteristics. Some involved collective action, others individual participation. A few situations took more time than others, three situations involved the risk of sanctions (demonstration). The implication of the various dimensions will be discussed later.

It is difficult, of course, to capture the richness of the natural setting in a written description. Let us take as an example the following situation which includes university authority and the voting strategy:

> Classified military research has been a controversial issue for some time. The question of whether or not it is legitimate to have secret military research at this university has been placed on the ballot for the next student election. All students are being urged to vote to express their opinion to the Regents on this matter.[2]

After reading this description of the situation, the person was asked a series of questions to elicit whether he/she 1) felt that the political authorities (Regents) would be responsive to this type of action on his part and 2) whether this action would be likely to increase his personal political influence on the authorities in question. In essence, they were asked the six general efficacy questions again, except that a different combination of political authority and strategy was inserted in the questions to correspond to the situation. This battery of six situational efficacy questions was asked after the exposure to each situation, and formed the situation efficacy measure.*

One example of the difference between a general efficacy and a situational question is as follows:

General efficacy: I believe public officals care what people like me want.

Situational efficacy: If I were to vote on this issue,** I believe that Regents would care what people like me want.[3]

---

*The questionnaire took between 35 and 50 minutes to answer. A longer instrument was used during the initial pretests, but it was subsequently shortened to reduce fatigue. In the final test instrument the difference in the percentage of no answers between the first and last part of the questionnaire was less than 2 percent.

**The situation was the one described on page 6 concerning classified military research on campus.

After each person responded to the situational efficacy scale, he was asked if he would participate in this situation and "why?"[4]

To summarize, respondents were exposed to the various stimuli, and measures were taken in the following sequence:
1. General efficacy, political awareness and interest, background data
2. Situation
3. Situational efficacy
4. Situational participation
5. Questions about the respondent's past situational participation and his awareness of the participation of others in a similar situation.

Sample Characteristics:

The theoretical questions we raise require that 1) the political issues woven through the situations be central to the subjects being studied, 2) there be sufficient variance on different modes of political participation and 3) variance on prior political participation. The cost of a national sample that included adequate numbers of these types would be prohibitively large.

The students in this sample were a demographic elite.[5] At most, they were also an emergent political elite, or at least members of that strata in the United States frequently referred to as the attentive public.

The students' ages ranged from 18 to 50, but 89 percent were from 19 to 23 years old. Sixty-nine percent were male. Eighty-eight percent were juniors or seniors (3.5 percent were graduates), practically all received their B.A.s in 1973 or 1974. The respondents were predominantly offspring of the upper middle class. Sixty-one percent came from families where father was either a professional, manager, or proprietor. The sample is typical, then, of the young adults who received their Liberal Arts degrees from one of the top five or six universities in the nation in the last six years.

Lester Milbrath would call the majority political "spectators." A disproportionate number, however, were "political gladiators." All had taken at least one upper division Political Science course. Ninety-two percent voted for president in the 1972 presidential election. Seventy-three percent reported reading newspaper articles about public affairs and politics "almost daily."* Other activity

---

*The student daily newspaper is widely read and gives a more comprehensive political coverage than the town newspaper.

included: writing letters to national officials suggesting some action to be taken (33%), joining a national demonstration in Washington (23%) and at the local level (24%).[6]

We wanted to see how typical the responses of subjects in this study were of a subset of the national population with similar demographic characteristics. Fortunately, at the same time that this research was being conducted, the Center for Political Studies at the University of Michigan was in the field with its study of voting behavior in the 1972 presidential election. From their national probability sample of 2705 adults, we selected two subgroups. The first included those respondents 18 years of age and older who graduated from a four year college and whose father was either a professional, proprietor, official or manager. Six percent of the national sample fit this rarified demographic mold. The second group was similar to the first except it was restricted to those from 18 to 30 years of age (2% of the national sample).

Although it proved impossible to examine every indicator, the national sample did include some items that were comparable; and as we see in Table 4.1, the young adults in the two populations are not far apart. Each sample was asked about its interest in politics. We know from past studies that Americans are generally more interested in national than local politics. Therefore, more university students should be in the higher ranges of the interest scale as they reported their interest in national politics (and local and university),[7] while the national sample was asked if it was interested in and followed government and public affairs in general.[8]

A second set of questions asked about newspaper and television usage. The national sample told how often they read newspaper articles about the *election*; university students reported how often they read newspaper articles more generally on public affairs and politics. Because there are political stimuli in the media beyond the election, this restriction may have lowered the affirmative responses somewhat in the national population. Under this assumption, we combined the two highest response categories in the national sample.[9] As one can see, only a few percentage points separated the two populations as they followed politics in the newspaper or TV.[10]

The last two questions were almost identical in both populations. Presidential voting behavior was similar for the three groups. The second question asked the members of each group if they had ever written a letter to a public official advocating he take some action. Again the two younger cohorts were not far apart, although the national population was slightly more active.[11]

TABLE 4.1

Comparison of the Political Interest and Participation of the Students with Two Age Groups of a National Sample Who Completed College and Whose Fathers Were Either Professionals, Managers, Officials or Proprietors.

	Interest in National Politics or Government and Politics Generally
Students	%
very interested	80
interested	19
National	
18-30	
most time	62
some time	34
18+	
most time	60
some time	31
	Read Newspapers about Public Affairs and Politics or about the National Campaign
Students	%
almost daily	73
National	
18-30	
regularly or often	65
18+	
regularly or often	68
	TV, Watch Programs about Public Affairs and Politics or the National Campaign
Students	%
almost daily	46
National	
18-30	
a good many	40
18+	
a good many	35
	Voted for President in 1972
Students	%
yes	92
National	
18-30	88
18+	92
	Letter to Public Official
Students	%
yes	33
National	
18-30	42
18+	53

CAUTIONARY NOTE

A quasi-experimental design inevitably introduces some measure of artificiality. Two possible effects could be the maximization of situation influence (B, Figure 4.1) and the minimization of the effect of general political efficacy (A, Figure 4.1).

Maximizing Situations:

The potency of situations will depend in part on the range of difference encapsulated in the situation. If people perceive all the situations to be quite similar, context will account for less variance in observed behavior. As an example of how choice of situations will influence results, let us say we are studying anxiety. Two hypotheses are being considered: anxiety reflects underlying personality dimensions, anxiety reflects situational effect. In time 1 we measure the personality traits which the literature tells us underlie anxiety. In time 2 we observe the subject being confronted and threatened by a motorcycle gang at dusk on a lonely country road. Next we observe him in the broad daylight crossing a moderately travelled street with the red light, accompanied by three close friends. In both situations we measure his anxiety level. The question is, do situations or personality best predict anxiety? Without doubt, personality would come in a poor second. Too extreme? Let us substitute for the motorcycle gang, then, running out of gas on a dark country road and having to walk two miles to the nearest house. Situation still may be a more influential predictor but we suspect the gap has been narrowed. Finally we shall replace the motorcycle gang with crossing a moderately travelled street, without the benefit of a traffic light, with friends in broad daylight. The difference between the situations is now reduced to the presence of a traffic light. Clearly the ability of "situations" to explain anxiety will be considerably curtailed. There are two observations we can make about the above example. The selection of situations in the first instance is an important determinant of the power of situations to explain behavior. Second, situational stimuli shape individual emotional states, and it is a wonder that personalogists excluded them for so long from their study of anxiety.[1,2]

The situations used in this study were selected with the help of the pretested population. We only selected realistic strategies. Reality in this instance was determined by the respondents who pointed out those strategies most commonly available to American citizens. We also restricted ourselves to situational characteristics which practically all the respondents had personally or vicariously experienced. This still means, however, that by including demonstrations, campaigns, and voting among the different situational characteristics, we were probably setting by some degree the potential limits of situational influence. That these limits were broader than one might find with another selection could be seen when we chose strategies routinely surveyed in election studies, most of which could be lumped under *campaign* activity. For example, we might include wearing a campaign button, passing out campaign literature, giving campaign contributions, and talking to friends about candidates. Unless other characteristics of the situations allied with these strategies were significantly different, we would not expect as wide a variation in the respondents' expectations as to the possible influence of these different strategies.

Another factor which could influence the impact of situations is the use of a written description of a situation rather than the richness of a natural setting. The suspicion that this may mute the effect of situations is supported by Bowers who surveyed the impact of different research designs on the relative influence of situations and personal differences. Although the number of studies in psychology available for this survey was small, self reports in quasi-experimentally induced situations (as in the present study) showed less weighty situational effects than in studies where the actual behavior of the individual was observed in a natural setting by a third person.[13]

Minimizing General Political Efficacy:

Earlier we saw that this sample of young adults looked much like a national sample of the attentive public. This still leaves open the possibility that the range of general political efficacy (GPE) is more truncated in the test population than it is for a similar slice of the national population. We assume it is even more likely when compared with the total adult population. If the range of GPE were reduced in the student sample its effect on participation would be restricted. To put the question more precisely, by what fraction is GPE's variance in the test population less than its variance in a similar slice of the national population and in the total adult population?[14]

The national election study (1972) asked four questions which are similar to general efficacy questions used in this study. Table 4.2 displays these distributions for the sample of young adults, comparable age subsets of the national population, and the total national election sample. Because of slight changes in wording and the fact that the responses from the national election sample were coded agree-disagree while the test sample responded on a five point Likert scale, the following comparison of the general efficacy ranges will be approximate. However, it will alert us when we attempt to generalize from the findings in Chapters 5 and 6 to other populations.

In order to grasp the relative truncation of GPE across the populations we calculated a distribution score for each frequency. This was the ratio of the smallest of each agree-disagree category to the largest. The closer the score to zero the more restricted the range of responses of the corresponding population to that general efficacy question. Let us use a difference greater than one tenth as an arbitrary indication of a significant difference between the scores. Table 4.2 shows that in three of four questions the variance in efficacy of the test population was equal to or less restricted than its variance in a comparative subset of the national population (18-30, 18+). However, when compared to the total national population, the range of responses of the test sample was more restricted in three of four cases. The gap in each instance was about .3.

Other things being equal, this implies that when we compare the test and target population (young adult members of the attentive public) the influence of GPE should be approximately the same. However, those who wish to generalize the results of this study to the total adult population in the United States should expect political efficacy to play a more important role in promoting political participation.

Having reviewed some of the potential problems inherent in studies of this type, we shall proceed to examine the limits of the proposition that general political efficacy is a personality disposition which is generalizable across situations.

TABLE 4.2
Minimizing General Political Efficacy, Comparison of Four Population Groups

	Ratio[a] of 1/3 or 3/1	1 Agree	2 Neither[b]	3 Disagree
1)				
Sample	.8	38%	14%	48%
18 - 30[d]	.2	14		86
18+	.2	14		86
Total population[c]	.7	41		59
2)				
Sample	.03	3	9	88
18 - 30	.9	48		52
18+	.8	45		55
Total population	.3	74		26
3)				
Sample	.7	31	25	44
18 - 30	.3	26		74
18+	.4	29		71
Total population	1.0	50		50
4)				
Sample	.6	48	21	31
18-30	.7	58		42
18+	.5	68		32
Total population	.9	47		53

[a] Ratio of the smallest of the agree-disagree categories to the largest.

[b] The questions in the test sample were coded on a five point Likert scale. In order to compare them with the agree-disagree codes of the national sample, agree "strongly" and "somewhat" were collapsed into agree and disagree "somewhat" and "strongly" were collapsed into disagree.

[c] The four statements that the national election sample were asked to agree with are:

"People like me don't have any say in what government does."

"Sometimes politics and government seem so complicated that a person like me really cannot understand what is going on."

"I don't think public officials care much what people like me think."

"The average citizen can have an influence in governmental decisions."

The last question was asked of one half of the split national sample. The four questions correspond to questions 6, 5, 1 and 4 of the test population, respectively. See footnote number 1, Chapter 4.

[d] The 18-30 and 18+ year olds are subsets of the 1972 national election sample. Each subset graduated from a four year college and had a father who was either a professional, proprietor, official or manager. "Total population" refers to the complete adult national election sample.

FOOTNOTES AND REFERENCES

[1] The following six questions constitute the general political efficacy scale (GPE). The items are identical or similar to the political efficacy questions used commonly in the literature. The items were selected to tap the notion that an individual citizen can influence political authority, that these officials will be responsive to his demands. For similar questions see David Easton and Jack Dennis, "The Child's Acquisition of Regime Norms," *The American Political Science Review* 61 (March, 1967), 29 and Angus Campbell, Gerald Gurin and Warren Miller, *The Voter Decides* (Evanston, Illinois: Row, Peterson 1954), 187-188.

Respondents recorded their answers to each question on a five point Likert scale:
1. I believe public officials care what people like me want.
2. If political authorities say they will do something you can depend on them to keep their word.
3. I think public officials consider most political matters to be too complicated for me to have an informed opinion.
4. I have some influence on what government does.
5. Politics and government seem so complicated that I really don't understand what's going on.
6. I feel incapable of having an impact on what political authorities do.

[2] During pretests we tried to determine the political issues at the university, local and national level in which students were most interested. At that time Vietnam, racial discrimination, ROTC, military research on campus, and marijuana headed the list. When one of these issues was woven through a situation, care was taken not to specify the position of the authority(s) on the issue. Students were told to assume that the position of the authority was the *opposite* of theirs.

Those who are interested in a description of all the situations used should contact the author. Examples of other situations are as follows:

"...a recent conviction of a local high school teacher for the possession of marijuana has led the Mayor to take a clear stand on legalizing the possession and use of marijuana in the city. You oppose his position and you are considering writing a letter to the Mayor expressing your views on the issue."

"The White House recently announced its policy on the wars in Vietnam and Cambodia and future United States involvements of this kind. You oppose the position of the White House. You

Cognitive Processes And The Inclusion of Situations 79

are asked by a group of people whom you know with the same opinions as yours to accompany them to Washington, D.C., to picket the White House. You are trying to decide whether to join the group."

[3] The following six statements (questions) were given to each respondent after exposure to every situation. Only the authority and strategy were changed.

"Circle the number which best reflects your feelings in the situation after EACH of the following statements."

	Agree strongly			Disagree strongly	
1. If I were to vote on this issue, I believe the Regents would care what people like me wanted.	1	2	3	4	5
2. If the Regents say they will do something as the result of this vote, I can depend on them keeping their word.	1	2	3	4	5
3. Even if I were to vote, I think the Regents generally consider this issue to be too complicated for me to have an informed opinion.	1	2	3	4	5
4. If I were to vote on this issue, it would have some influence on the Regents' decision.	1	2	3	4	5
5. Student elections are so complicated that I really don't understand enough to vote.	1	2	3	4	5
6. I feel incapable of having an impact on the Regents' decision in this matter by voting.	1	2	3	4	5

The six items formed an acceptable Guttman scale after each of the situations. The lowest coefficient of reproducability among the fifteen situational efficacy scales was .93.

Because we were concerned about possible test contamination between the general efficacy questions asked in section 1 and the situational questions in section 2 of the questionnaire, three matched groups of students were tested with different placement of the general efficacy questions. Group A received the general efficacy questions in the first section of the questionnaire as required by the research design. Group B had the questions placed at the end of the instrument, after their situational efficacy had been measured, Group C received nó general efficacy questions. The differences were slight. The situational efficacy of those that received the general efficacy questions first was on the average about 2 percent lower than Group B. For no situation did the difference between groups A and B rise above 4.1 percent. The average situational efficacy of group C was 0.5 percent higher than Group B.

For these reasons we felt confident that prior exposure to the general efficacy questions did not significantly bias the respondents' situational efficacy scores.

[4] We were concerned about the possible unwanted interaction between exposure to *written* situational efficacy questions and the measure of participation. Respondents exposed to the situation could calculate their political confidence without being prodded by the situational efficacy questions. The presentation of the situational efficacy statements could act as a goad and produce artificially higher rates of political participation than one would expect normally.

To examine the extent of the problem, two matched groups were tested. Group A was exposed to the situation and asked if it would participate; no situational efficacy questions were asked. Group B was given the situation, situation efficacy questions, and the question about participation. The participation rates of Group B were higher, but only about 2.5 percent on the average. Therefore, we felt that prior exposure to the situational efficacy questions was not artificially raising the participation score to any significant degree.

[5] The sample strategy is similar to what has been called "scope sampling." Our concern was more with the relationship between the variables than with accurate estimates of a broad national population. Generality lies in the reproducability of the findings both in Political Science and Social Psychology.

Through pretests we learned what the general levels of politicization and issue awareness were among students in the college. When it was clear that there would be sufficient variance on the variables in the model, we randomly selected a number of upper division courses in Political Science. All 530 students attending those courses were given questionnaires; 510 returned completed schedules.

⁶ Because we were examining people in situations which involved political issues, influence strategies and different levels of political authority, it was vital to know just how politicized these students were. To subject students to situations in which they would have little interest would have increased the artificiality of the test. During the pretest we tried to find out which issues were of most concern. These issues were used in the test situations. Also each student in the test was asked if he/she had heard the particular issue discussed by family, friends or the media. Then they were asked if they were interested in the issue themselves. Not surprisingly, a low of 92% said they had heard either their families, friends or the media discuss the Vietnam War, legalization of marijuana, a quota system to eliminate discrimination against hiring minorities and women, and the question of having secret military research on campus. A low 82% expressed interest in each of these issue areas.

Students were also asked their overall interest in politics at the national, city and university level as well as how much they had heard about election campaigns in the three areas. Seventy-eight percent said they had heard friends, family or the media discuss election campaigns at the university level. The figure rises to 95 and 99 percent as we moved to city and national election campaigns. The study was conducted just after the presidential election in 1972. Ninety-nine, 78 and 50 percent of the students expressed a general interest in national, city and university politics, respectively. Evidently, these students were more interested in specific issues related to the university than in university politics in general.

Measures of the centrality of politics and the issues were constructed for each level of authority. Significant differences will be reported. The reader should be aware, however, that the sample is divided essentially between those with very high and high concern.

⁷ The response categories were "very interested, interested, not very interested, not interested at all."

⁸ The response categories were "most of the time, some of the time, only now and then, hardly at all."

⁹ The response categories for the student sample were "almost daily, two or three times a week, two or three times a month, less than once a month." The response categories for the national sample were "regularly, often, time to time, once in a great while."

For both media questions the national sample was split and only 1333 persons were asked.

¹⁰ The response categories for newspapers and TV were similar for students. People in the national sample reported how many TV programs on the election campaign they watched: "a good many, several, just one or two."

[11] Forty-eight percent of the students reported they had worked in some capacity in one of the national political campaigns. There was not a comparable question in the national sample. However, 55% of the 18-30 year olds in the national sample said that during the recent campaigns they had tried to "help a party or candidate win..." by talking to people and trying to "show them" whom they should vote for and why.

[12] Most psychologists and certainly every scholar we quoted or cited in Chapter 1 has been aware of the potential importance of situations. Often this is forcefully brought home to us as we review the unexplained residual variance in our data. Faced with the complexity of situations, however, we opted to follow the course of least methodological resistance and emphasize attitudes and dispositons. At an early juncture in the research process this was a wise and efficient research strategy, for it meant parsimony in number of predictors and manageability of design. Yet what at one point in the history of ideas may be a virtue, can become an entrapment with continued replication. For research procedures have a way of dictating the theoretical questions we raise.

For earlier examples of the theoretical interest in situations as well as dispositions by political scientists see Robert Lane, *Political Life* (Glencoe: Free Press, 1959), 99-100; Angus Campbell, Philip E. Converse, Warren E. Miller and Donald Stokes, *The American Voter* (New York: John Wiley, 1960) 500; Fred Greenstein, "The Impact of Personality on Politics: An Attempt to Clear Away the Underbrush," *American Political Science Review* 61 (September 1967), 629-641; *Personality and Politics: Problems of Evidence, Inference and Conceptualization* (Chicago: Markham, 1969). For an excellent summary of the conceptual issues as well as the literature in personality and politics see Fred I. Greenstein, "Personality and Politics," in Fred I. Greenstein and Nelson W. Polsby (eds.) *Handbook of Political Science* (Mass.: Addison-Wesley, 1975) Vol. 2, Chapter 1.

[13] Kenneth Bowers, "Situationism in Psychology, an Analysis and Critique," *Psychological Review* 80 (September, 1973), 322, Table 2.

[14] Philip Converse brought this problem to my attention.

Chapter 5

POLITICAL EFFICACY: STABLE DISPOSITION OR CHANGING COGNITIVE BELIEF

This chapter focuses on the third link (A) in the psychodynamic model (G→ A→ F) and the assumption that psychological dispositions such as political efficacy are stable across situations. To begin this analysis we examine two hypotheses concerning efficacy.

Hypothesis 1:

If political efficacy is a global disposition reflecting enduring dimensions of the human personality, then a prior measure of one's general political efficacy should be a strong predictor of the same person's political confidence (situational efficacy, SE) across a variety of situations.

General efficacy (A, Figure 1.1) is associated with SE in the fifteen settings. Yet the magnitude of the overall relationship is not strong ($r = .28$). Knowing a person's general political efficacy (GPE) score explains less than 8 percent of the variance in SE. Disaggregating the fifteen situations does not strengthen the relationship appreciably. The amount of variance explained by individual difference never rises above 9 percent; nor is there a distinctive pattern between GPE and SE among the fifteen situations.

The magnitude of these relationships places in jeopardy an expected linkage that might have run from relevant past experience to GPE to SE (E→ A→ C, Figure 1.1). Thus even if individual differences are residues of past experience, the linkage to SE is weak, at best.

As one who has worked with psychological dispositions in my own past research, I confess to my initial concern with this finding. The trans-situational variation in dispositions has also been a source of concern for psychologists. Peterson laments:

the generality of these [personality] measures over method and situation was still not high enough to justify perpetuating the traditional conceptions of personality.... The findings required abandonment of a line of research to which I devoted ten years of my life as a psychologist. The results also required a change in beliefs about the nature of personality. This research, per se, did not say which way the conceptual shift should go, but it suggested very strongly that traditional conceptions of personality as internal behavior dispositions were inadequate and insufficient.[1]

Hypothesis 2:

The treatment of political efficacy as a stable psychological disposition also means that if we follow the *same person* across the fifteen situations, each time measuring his political efficacy (SE) in that situation, there should be little variation.

In order to display the data in a clear and parsimonious form the SE of the sample in each situation was converted into a percentage difference index (PDI). That is, the percentage who did not feel efficacious using a given strategy was subtracted from those who did feel confident in that situation. If, for example, 62 percent believed petitioning was a good way to influence university Regents while 38 percent did not, the PDI for that situation would be +24 (62 - 38 = 24). Theoretically the PDI can vary between +100 and -100. Negative values indicate the degree to which people do not feel efficacious.

Figure 5.1 plots the PDI for situational efficacy in fifteen situations characterized by the five strategies and three levels of political authority. Quite obviously SE varies considerably by both strategy and level. In national politics, SE changes from a relative euphoria with campaigning as a mode of political influence (PDI = +84) to a strong disenchantment with picketing in Washington (-70). Looking at these two extremes at the national level, the total PDI difference is 155. Clearly, people have a significant ability to discriminate between situations. The stimuli are not perceived as equivalent and situational efficacy changes accordingly. The influence of setting on SE in the city (80) and university (85) is also significant, if less extreme. The lack of consistency in efficacy scores across the fifteen situations reflects the +.30 ceiling on cross-situational correlation coefficients commonly observed in social psychology. The mean correlation in fifteen variable intercorrelation matrix of SE is .32.

Political Efficacy 85

FIGURE 5.1
Variation in Percentage Difference in Situational
Efficacy by Strategy and Level of Authority

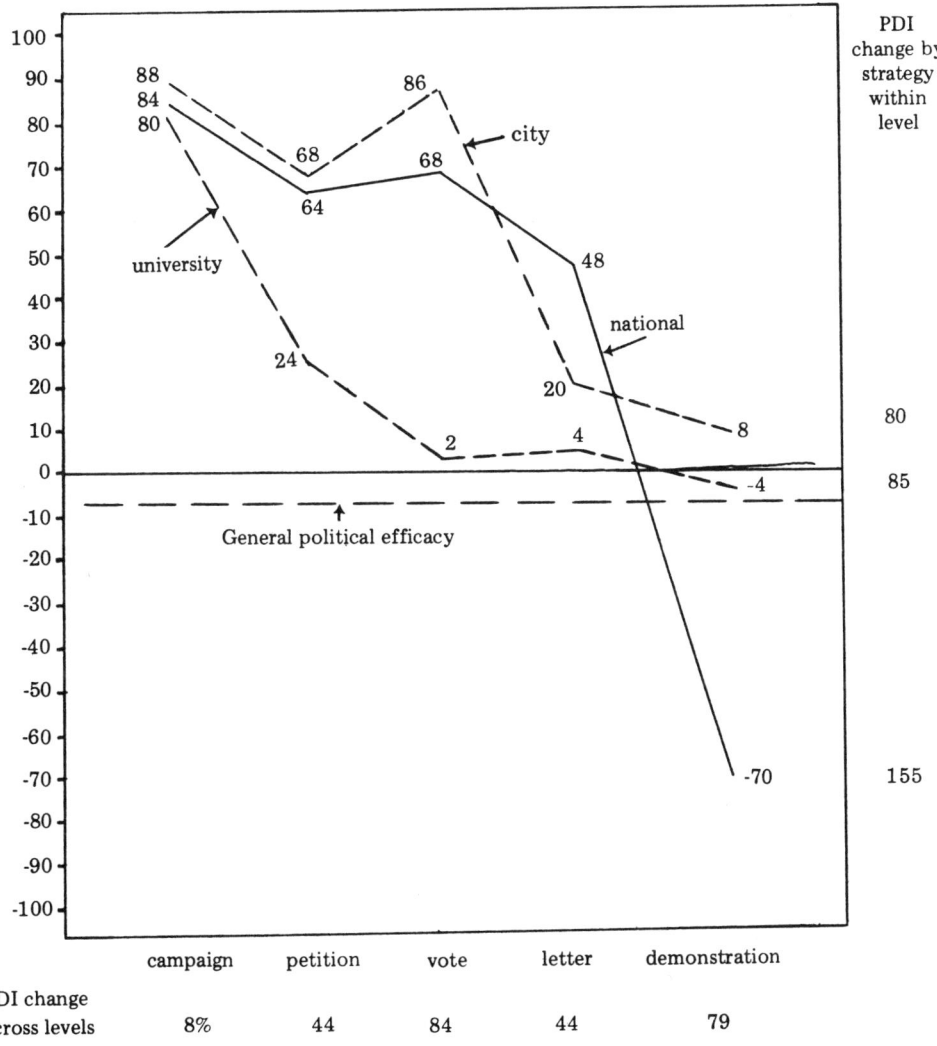

The PDI for general political efficacy was measured prior to people's entering the situations. It was -5. When we ask the general efficacy questions again in the situational context it is clear (from Figure 5.1) that knowing the GPE of an individual tells us little about how efficacious the same person is going to feel when he is considering the possibility of campaigning or demonstrating.

Situation efficacy also changes across levels, although the percentage change is lower than the change across strategies. The least dispersion in PDI is with campaigning (8 percent difference). Most people feel efficacious about their campaigning at all levels. They also are confident about voting and petitioning in city and national politics. They see public officials as being least responsive to letters and public demonstrations. Overall, they have less confidence about the impact of any of these strategies at the university level. But even here there is considerable variation across settings. Recent and past evidence of vote fraud, as well as allegations of corruption leveled against the last two governments of the Student Governing Association has helped reduce students' sense that voting at the university is a very effective way to influence university policy.

Aside from the impact of strategy and level, there are other characteristics that cut across the fifteen situations. One such dimension is individual versus collective action. People may feel more confident about their personal political influence if they are a part of a group or collective attempt, rather than acting as individuals. This generalization is not reflected in the data. People are most pessimistic about demonstrations while they feel very confident about campaign strategies; both are forms of collective action (along with petitioning). Nor is SE the same for the two individual strategies. They are relatively efficacious about voting (except in university politics) but much less so about letter writing.

Another dimension involves sanctions and the possible commission of illegal acts. Although peaceful assembly and demonstration are guaranteed by the Constitution, SE was lowest in situations involving demonstrations. This is not surprising considering, for example, that 65 percent of the group that had demonstrated against national authorities felt their activity had had no impact. No one believed that it had "a lot" of influence. Nor were they encouraged by what they heard from others. Fifty-three percent of those who had heard about others engaging in this type of political expression felt it had had absolutely no effect. Only 3 percent believed it had "a lot" of influence.

After the respondents made their participation decisions they were asked "why" they would or would not participate in the demonstration. A continuous thread at each level was the mention of sanctions and presumed illegality. Another line of argument was that demonstrations would only "turn off" the officials; they would become "defensive." Apparently demonstrations and picketing are often considered illegal, even when they are not. Certainly one runs the risk of being imprisoned or injured for participating in such activity. This can serve as a considerable deterrent, if not to one's confidence, at least to the willingness to accept these risks by joining a demonstration. Yet such arguments never accompanied the decisions on voting and campaigning, norms which receive considerable support in the political culture of the United States.

Those who are interested in keeping open all constitutionally guaranteed channels of political expression may be particularly alarmed by these responses. These respondents are members of the attentive public. Many have tried in the past to express themselves politically through demonstrations. Forty-six percent of the sample had demonstrated at the university, one quarter in the city, and 23 percent in Washington, D.C.

A final dimension in the situations is issue area. Four different issues* are woven through the settings. Possibly this could cause variations in SE. Yet we know from the test and the pretest, that on a single issue the SE of politically concerned respondents will change as they consider different strategies. For example, the data for demonstrations at the city and national level focus on one issue while unversity demonstration incorporates a different issue. As you can see (Figure 5.1), the difference in SE toward demonstrations at the city and national level (same issue) is greater than the difference between either and SE toward demonstrations (different issue) in the university. Issues do not give us much of a hold on the pattern in Figure 5.1.

Further understanding of the changes in SE comes from the appreciation that situational context combines not only the contemporaneous stimuli but the prior situational learning that people bring to the immediate setting. Take someone, for example, who sat in at an ROTC building in the past and only received a record for criminal trespass for his efforts.[2] When confronted with a similar situation, he is likely to take a jaundiced view toward extending his police record further (Figure 1.1, E x B→ C).

After each situation we asked the respondent if he had in the past used this strategy at the same level of authority. In order to gain

---

*Vietnam war, legalization of marijuana, secret military research and quota systems (racial discrimination).

some understanding of the meaning the subjects gave this past stimulus, we also asked if they felt that their past action had had "no," "some" or "a lot" of influence on the officials in question.

Figures 5.2-4 show that past experience does combine with the contemporary stimuli to influence one's SE. Stimuli in each situation acted as a cue to those who had used a strategy before and felt it had "a lot" of influence. Past experience helped shape their expectancy about outcomes in the current situation. At the same time, the people who felt their prior action had "no influence" were consistently less confident. For some situations the differences were greater than 90 PDI's.

There still is considerable variation in SE across the settings, although it is reduced at the national and city level for those who believe their past situational participation had a lot of influence. Prior learning has its smallest impact in campaigning situations. Even those who felt they campaigned before without effect are not deterred from placing their political confidence in campaigning in the present.

The effect of past participation on SE is also reduced in the voting situation at the city level (Figure 5.3). This can be explained in part by the presence of a radical and viable third party in the city. This party had two members on the city council and ran candidates in every ward. Many of the respondents who in the past had participated in an election in their home towns may have been frustrated by the lack of candidates with views close to their own. Even though they voted, they may have felt afterwards that it was to no avail. The local voting situation was not in their home towns, but in three-party university city where they resided. Although they felt their past votes in another locale had "no influence," they may have felt quite differently in this new situation with a wider array of candidates and parties from which to choose.

We have seen that past participation experience does interact with the present situation to affect one's situational efficacy. On the other hand, there were many people who had not participated in these situations. They had heard, however, about the experiences of others in similar situations. After each situation we asked each respondent if he had heard about others who had used this type of strategy to influence the same level of government. Those who had heard were asked if they believed the action of these other people had had "no," "some" or "a lot" of influence on the political officials. Just as past situational experience of self combines with the present setting, so should one's vicarious awareness of the experience of others interact with the current situation to affect SE (Figure 4.1, D x B→C).

Political Efficacy 89

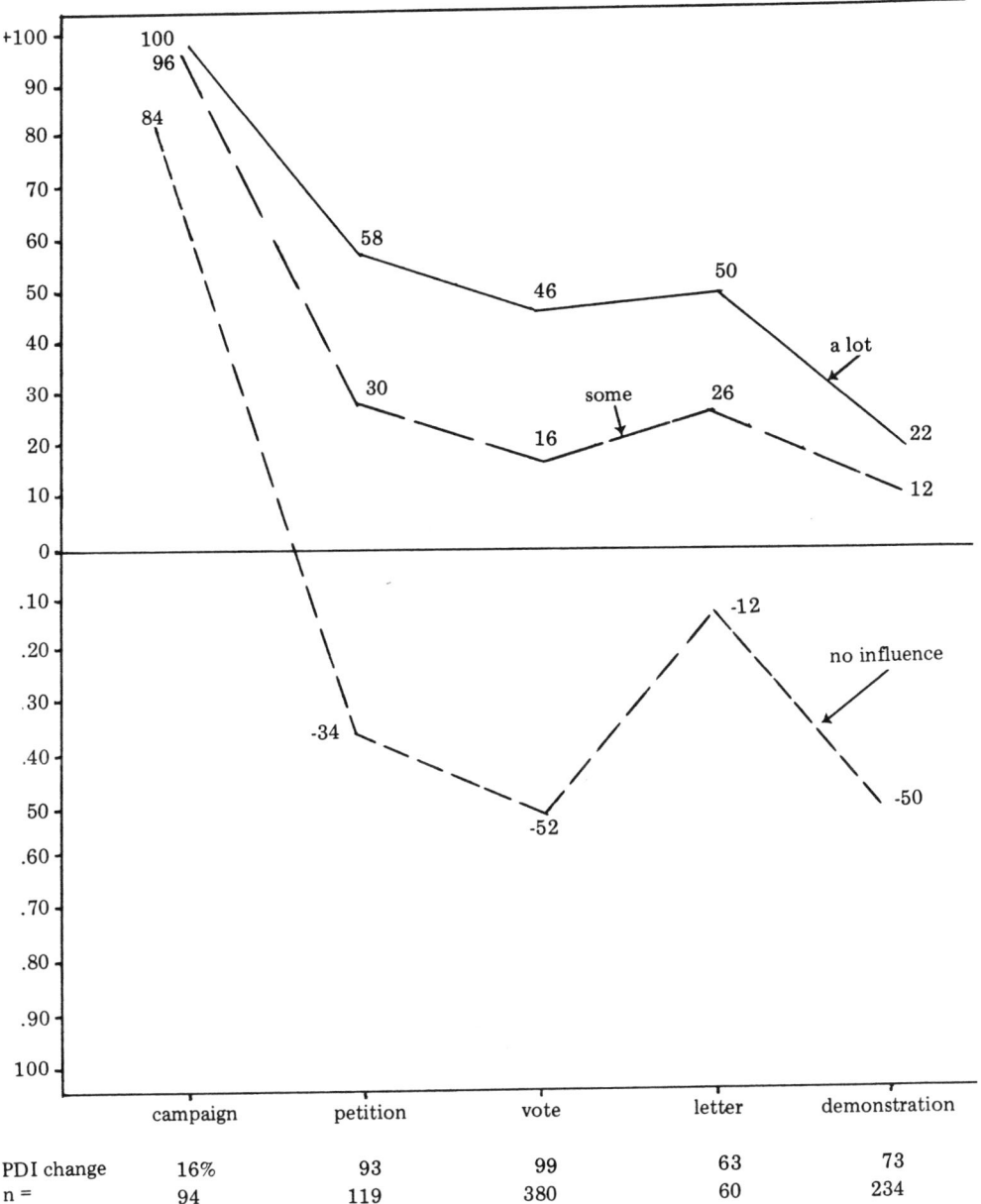

FIGURE 5.2

Variation in Percentage Difference in Situational Efficacy at the University Level by Strategy and Past Influence of Self in Similar Situations

90 Political Participation and Learning

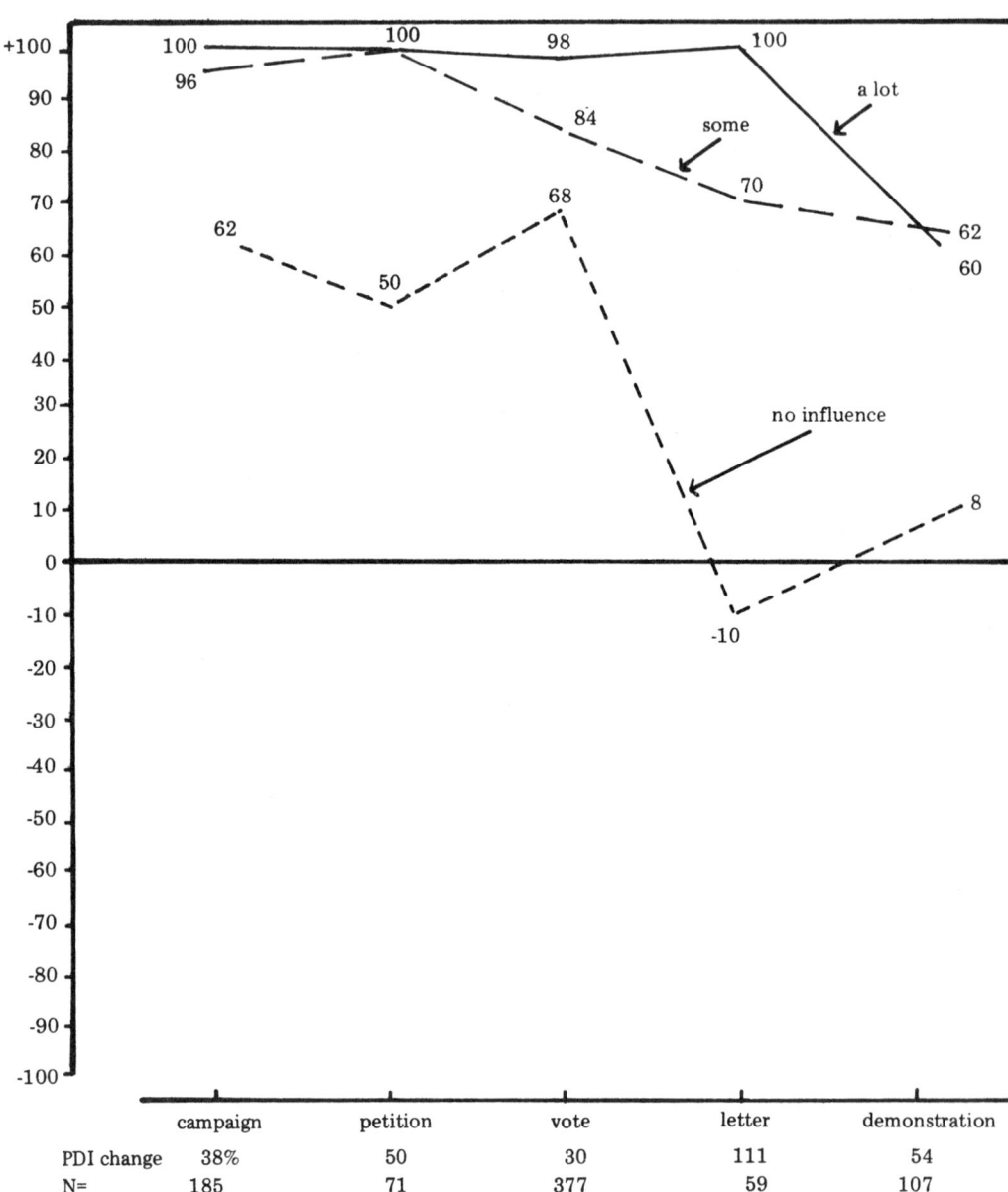

FIGURE 5.3
Variation in Percentage Difference in Situational Efficacy at the City Level by Strategy and Past Influence of Self in Similar Situations

Political Efficacy 91

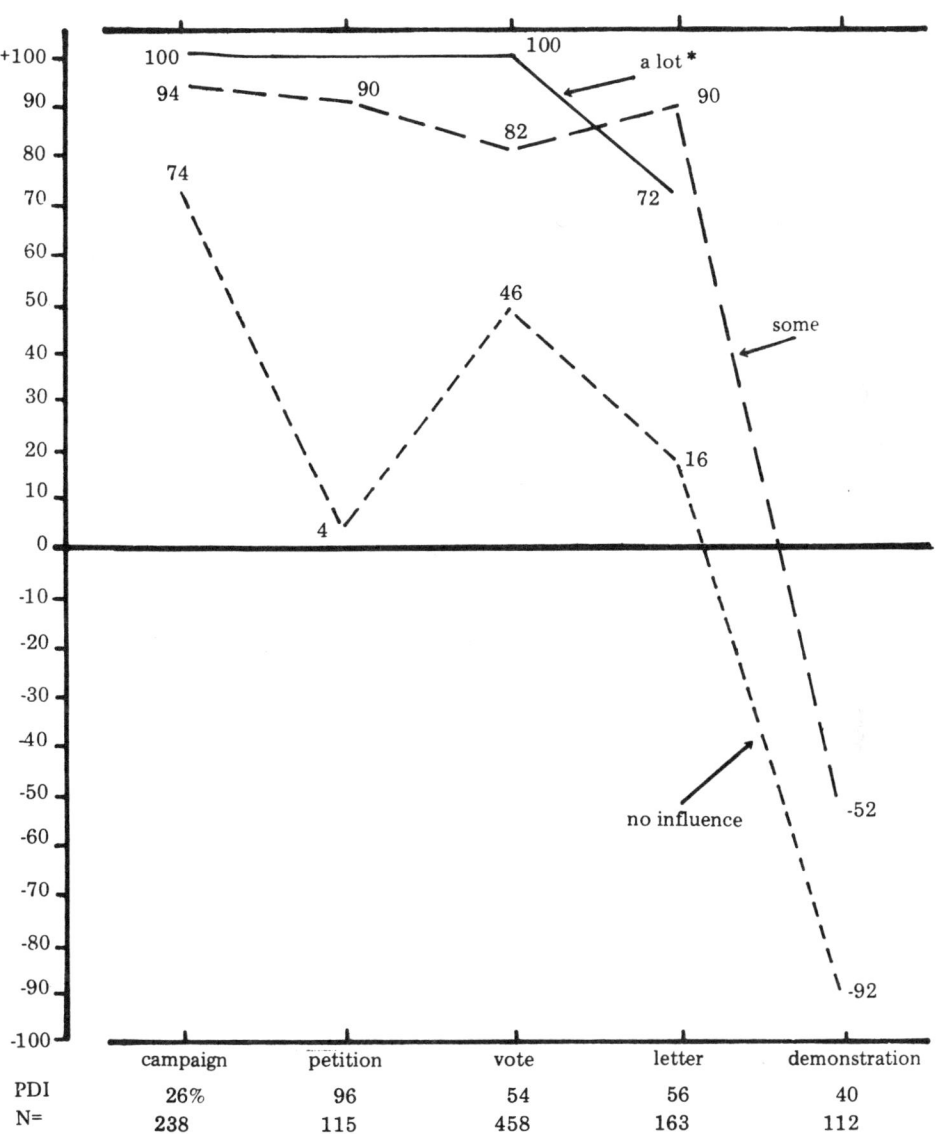

FIGURE 5.4

Variation in Percentage Difference in Situational Efficacy at the National Level by Strategy and Past Influence of Self in Similar Situations

*No one who had demonstrated in Washington before felt it had had a lot of influence.

Those who were aware of other people successfully using the same strategy to influence public officials were consistently more efficacious when confronted with a similar situation. People who felt that the activity of "others" had had no influence always had significantly lower SE in similar settings.

To summarize, we cannot confirm the second hypothesis since there is considerable change in SE as we observe people across different situations. Both the respondent's past experience and his vicarious awareness of the experience of others interact with the current situational stimuli to change SE. Overlaying the relation between prior learning and SE is (1) the consistently lower SE of people in university politics (except campaigning), (2) the smaller relation between prior learning and SE in campaigning situations and (3) the lower SE throughout of those facing the possibility of engaging in a political demonstration.

Four Predictors of Situational Efficacy:

It is clear at this point that situational efficacy cannot be explained entirely by personality theory (general political efficacy) nor by a stimulus-response process set off by the situation (B-C, Figure 4.1). To these two variables we must add perceptions of past learning of self in corresponding settings, and what we learned from the experience of others. Moreover, we have suggested that the *interactions* between these four predictors make a significant contribution to one's belief that he can or cannot influence public officials.

To obtain a surer grasp of the location of the interactions we used the Automatic Interaction Detector 3 program to search and structure the four predictor variables.[3] The AID 3 program incorporates the familiar "tree" analysis which orders explanatory variables hierarchically by their importance in accounting for variance in the dependent variable. If the predictors interact, this is apparent from the computer printout.

AID showed considerable interaction. While it did not indicate the amount of variance in political participation explained by interaction, it did point to the need for a form of multivariate analysis which accounts for the influence of interactions as well as the independent effect of each of the predictors on SE.

For the final stage of the analysis we used MANOVA.[4] This is a multifactor analysis of variance program which accepts categorical variables. It allows one to assess the relative direct contribution of each explanatory variable and their interactions to the variance in situational efficacy.[5]

MANOVA assumes the dependent variable is an interval measure.

Situational efficacy is a seven-point Guttman scale. Although we should not be hesitant in making "less than, greater than" statements about the relationships, interval statements should be taken with more caution.[6]

Because of the 80 cell limitation in the MANOVA program, we divided situations into national, city and university. This removes situational variation across levels of government. But situations, as we shall see, still contribute to people's political confidence.*

Tables 5.1-3 show the direct effect of each of the four predictors, as well as the influence of their interactions, upon situational efficacy at each level of government. Only those who had participated in similar situations are included in the analysis. The reader should be aware that by selecting only those who have participated before, we have isolated a subset of the larger sample whose past situational experience has made more discriminating.** Their heightened cognitive sensitivity is likely to increase the number of significant interactions and augment the predictive power of the model.

Tables 5.1-3 show that interactions do indeed dominate the explanation of SE. The interactions which are associated with the most variance are between past situational experience of self or others and characteristics of the situation. General political efficacy has the least effect on SE. Yet in national and city politics, GPE contributes to interactions associated with 46 and 48 percent of the variance in SE, respectively.***

We also examined the impact of the four predictors with the entire sample. To do this it was necessary to drop the important information about whether the subject who had participated in a similar situation felt he had been influential. Instead, to include the whole sample, past participation of self (variable E in Figure 1.1) was dichotomized between those who had and had not participated in a similar situation. There were attendant consequences when less discriminating people who lacked prior political experience were added to the analysis. The number of interactions declined, and the explanatory power of the model was reduced (national, 53 percent of variance explained; city, 36 percent; and university, 54 percent). We shall look more closely at the impact of cognitive sensitivity when we examine the antecedents of political participation in the next chapter.

---

*The cell limitation also necessitated the collapsing of the general efficacy measure. But, as reported in Chapter 6, this had no significant effect on the results.
**Later we shall examine the entire sample.
***How much each predictor contributes to the interactions is discussed in Chapter 6.

TABLE 5.1

Variance in Situational Efficacy by National Situations, General Efficacy, Past Influence of Self in Similar Situations and Past Influence of Others in Similar Situations.

		Percent variance
A[a]	GPE	0[b]
B	Situations	6
D	Past influence of others	4
E	Past influence of self[c]	0
A x B x E		2
B x D x E		16
A x B x D x E		44
Error		28
Total variance explained[d]		72
N = 944[e]		

	Situations	Past Influence of others	Past Influence of self	GPE
Direct	6	4	0	0
Interaction	62	60	62	46
	68 [f]	64	62	46

a) The letters designating the variables in this and subsequent tables correspond to Figures 4.1 and 1.1 The order of variable entry in the MANOVA analysis is as listed.

b) Explained variance of less than .7 of one percent will be excluded from this and subsequent tables. In each case this residual variance will be added to error. In no table does this pooled variance account for more than four percent.

c) "E" measures the respondent's belief that his/her past participation had "a lot," "some" or "no" influence on the authorities in question.

d) In order to interpret the model presented the grand mean has been excluded from the final calculation of variance associated with the predictors, their interactions, and error.

e) Multiplying 15 situations by 510 subjects brings the total number of cases to be examined to 7650. Missing data, excluded data (those who did not participate in the situation before) and controls will reduce the actual N.

f) Proportion of the total variance explained (72%) to which the predictor is associated directly, and through interaction with the other predictors. This form of summation will be used in subsequent tables.

TABLE 5.2

Variance in Situational Efficacy by City Situations, General Efficacy, Past Influence of Self in Similar Situations and Past Influence of Others in Similar Situations

		Percent variance
A	GPE	0
B	Situations	0
D	Past influence of others	1
E	Past influence of self	0
A x D x E		2
B x D x E		31
A x B x D x E		46
Error		20
Total variance explained		80
N = 795		

	Past Influence of Others	Past Influence of self	Situations	GPE
Direct	1	0	0	0
Interaction	79	77	77	48
	80	77	77	48

In this chapter we found little evidence to support the hypothesis that a conventional measure of general political efficacy is a highly generalizable disposition. Knowing one's prior GPE tells us little about his efficacy level in situations where he must decide whether to participate in politics. Among the four predictors examined, GPE was the least effective in predicting situational efficacy. Although the generalizability of GPE was not strong enough to satisfy a traditional personality explanation of behavior, we shall see in Chapter 6 that the inclusion of such general measures will add usefully to our prediction of political participation.

In Chapter 3 we questioned the first and second links in the psychodynamic model that political confidence has exclusive roots in early learning. Here data on the attentive public casts doubt on the third link, that GPE is a personality disposition that renders situational stimuli functionally equivalent. In the next chapter we shall investigate the last link in the psychodynamic model: the impact of the GPE on the decision to participate in politics. This is done within a global examination of situational and cognitive processing predictors of political participation.

TABLE 5.3

Variance in Situational Efficacy by University Situations, General Efficacy, Past Influence of Self in Similar Situations and Past Influence of Others in Similar Situations

		Percent variance
A	GPE	0
B	Situations	2
D	Past influence of others	1
E	Past influence of self	0
A x B		1
A x D		12
B x E		9
D x E		3
A x B x D		2
A x B x E		13
B x D x E		14
A x B x D x E		17
Error		26
Total variance explained		74
N = 707		

	Situations	Past Influence of Self	Past Influence of others	GPE
Direct	2	0	1	0
Interaction	68	56	48	33
	70	56	49	33

FOOTNOTES AND REFERENCES

[1] Donald R. Peterson, *The Clinical Study of Social Behavior* (New York: Appleton-Century Crofts, 1968), 23. Also cited in Kenneth Bowers, "Situationism in Psychology, An Analysis and Critique," *Psychological Review* 80 (September, 1973), 319.

[2] In past years students struggled with university authorities over the issue of establishing a university bookstore run by the students. The political conflict culminated in the seizure of the Administration Building by the students. After considerable hesitation, the university authorities finally asked the police to break up the sit-in. Students were arrested and charged. Some were acquitted, others now have criminal records. This incident continues to be a part of the political culture of the more politically attentive students, even though they were not personally involved in the sit-in themselves.

[3] John Sonquist, Elizabeth Lauh Baker and James Morgan, *Searching for Structure* (Ann Arbor, Michigan: Institute for Social Research, University of Michigan, 1973).

[4] This version of the OSIRIS MANOVA program was developed by Charles E. Hall and Elliot M. Cramer. It was modified by Neal Van Eck of the Survey Research Center, Institute for Social Research, University of Michigan. Unfortunately, there is no single ideal reference to this program. Interested readers should consult the "MANOVA Write-Up" of the program at I.S.R.

[5] We will also use MANOVA in Chapter 6 to examine the antecedents of political participation.

[6] Because of the purposive nature of the sample little claim can be made for the statistical generality of the results.

Chapter 6

DECISION TO PARTICIPATE IN POLITICS

Up to this point we have focused on links in the psychodynamic model which were a step removed from political participation. This chapter examines the effect of general political efficacy, the immediate situation, situational efficacy, and past learning on the decision to participate. It presumes that decisions to participate are a part of a cognitive learning process in which stimuli in the present situation act as a cue for the individual. They help shape his expectancy about possible outcomes in the immediate situation (SE) based on what he has learned before in similar situations. The subject is perceiving the situation, generalizing from past experiences, and making decisions in a system in which the different predictors are interacting.

INTRODUCTION

The political participation on which this chapter focuses includes the willingness of people to vote, campaign, petition, write letters and demonstrate. We measured people's behavior intention rather than observing their actual participation.[1] However, we saw in Chapter 4 that the level of participation of this sample was not out of line with that of a similar subset of the national population. A third way to measure behavior is to collect self reports of past political participation. What effect might these three different measures of participation—behavior intention, observed participation and recollected behavior—have upon the strength of the attitude-behavior relationships we shall examine? Alan Liska reviewed a number of studies where these different measures of behavior had been employed. He concluded:

"While the strength of the relationships between attitudes and behavior differ somewhat from study to study, systematic differences between the three measurement categories do not appear."[2]

This does not mean, of course, that differences between the three measures are unimportant. It merely suggests that the impact of these differences upon attitude-behavior linkages may have been overemphasized.

There was considerable variation in willingness to participate. The highest rate was for voting in the national election. Eighty-two percent said definitely "yes" they would vote. The low was for sitting-in at the university; only 9 percent said they would definitely participate in that situation, an additional 22 percent said probably. Overall, behavior which carried the heaviest sanctions (demonstrations, sit-ins) had the fewest adherents, while those with the greatest cultural support—voting—attracted the largest number of participants. Voting was followed in order by campaigning, letter writing and petitioning. Overall participation rates were somewhat higher in situations dealing with national issues and politicians than in university or city situations.

Methodological Considerations:

As in Chapter 5 we employed AID 3 to structure the predictors of participation and test for their interactions. The MANOVA program was then used to examine the direct contribution of each of the five predictors[3] and their interactions to the variance in the decision to participate. As mentioned before, the 80 cell limit required some collapsing of the predictors. There was little collapsing that was required for the two measures of prior learning (self and through others). Our concern was with the two seven-point measures of SE and General Political Efficacy (GPE). Each had to be dichotomized. Although AID was used to determine the cutting points that would maximize the variance explained by each predictor, we also compared the difference between the expanded and collapsed versions of SE and GPE.

As one can see below, collapsing had no significant effect on GPE (Table 6.1). The variance explained was less than one percent in both cases. Collapsing did reduce by one percent the amount of variance in participation explained by SE. Overall, the collapsing of these two variables has a very small effect on their relation to participation.

TABLE 6.1

Variance in Decision to Participate
Explained by Two Versions of General
Political Efficacy and Situational Efficacy

		Collapsed	Entire Range
A	General political efficacy	1%	1%
C	Situational efficacy	5	6
A x C		0	0
Error		94	93
Total variance explained		6	7
N^a =		6717	6717

[a]Those respondents who were "unsure" if they would participate in the situation were excluded from the analysis.

GPE and SE do not by themselves account for much variance in participation. Yet if situations shape expectancies (SE) about outcomes, we would expect SE to be most influential in interaction with situations. This is clearly the case in Table 6.2 as SE directly accounts for only 4 percent of the variance in participation but contributes an additional 10 percent through second and third factor interactions with situations. Throughout the analysis we shall see that the principal influence of SE (and GPE) is through interaction with situations.

Situations are a necessary constituent of all interactions in Table 6.2. Directly and through interactions situational stimuli are associated with 32 percent of the total variance (36 percent) explained by this three-factor model.

POLITICAL PARTICIPATION: FIVE PREDICTORS AND THEIR INTERACTIONS

The cognitive processing approach assumes that a person's decision to participate is shaped by his expectancy about outcomes which interacts with situational stimuli and past learning. This interaction model requires the inclusion of past learning of self (Figure 1.1), others, situational efficacy, and situations. If we also add GPE, the 80 cell limitation of MANOVA requires the breaking of situations

TABLE 6.2

Variance in Decision to Participate Explained by Situations, Situational Efficacy and General Political Efficacy

		Percent of Variance
A	GPE	0
B	Situations	19
C	SE	4
A x B		3
A x C		0
B x C		6
A x B x C		4
Error		64
Total variance explained		36
N = 6717		

	Situations	SE	GPE
Direct	19	4	0
Interaction	13	10	7
	32	14	7

into national, city and university. This does remove some cross level variation in context. But, as we shall see, situations continue to play a central role in explaining the decision to participate at each level.

Cognitive Sensitivity:

As the learning process we are examining stresses interaction and cognition, the cognitive sensitivity of the respondents should significantly influence the working of the model. The past participation experience of the sample will give us some purchase on this question.

All subjects were asked if they had participated in a comparable situation before; in most cases the majority had not. There was a minority, however, who entered the new setting having already learned from a similar experience. It is this group who we might expect to be most discriminating in the present situation. If cognitive processing underlies the statistical interactions, the heightened cognitive awareness of this sub-group should increase the predictive power of the interaction model. Their increased discrimination should have another effect as well, to augment the number of significant interactions and the amount of variance explained by interaction. The explanation of behavior of the more discriminating person is complex, relatively specific to a number of predictors, and likely to be greatly determined by all of them.[4]

Tables 6.3-5 include only those persons who have had prior experience themselves in analogous situations. The variable being measured (E) is their belief that their participation had a lot, some or no influence on the authorities in question. A number of conclusions can be drawn from these three tables. First, the total amount of variance explained at the national (78 percent), city (70 percent) and university (81 percent) levels is relatively high compared with results from an enlarged sample which includes both those who have and have not had prior situational experience (Tables 6.6-8). Second, the primary effect of predictors is overshadowed by complex interactions. There is more interaction among this more cognitively sensitive group than among the enlarged sample where most had no prior experience with the situations (Tables 6.6-8).[5] Third, situations are a constituent of all interactions, except one, of any magnitude. Directly or through interactions, situations are consistently associated with greater variance in the decision to participate than the situation specific beliefs (SE), prior learning about the influence of self (E) or others (D), and genotypic dispositions such as general political efficacy. Fourth, situation efficacy, beliefs about influence of self and general political efficacy all contribute to interactions which explain a significant amount of variance in the decision to participate.

Among the more cognitively sensitive, the direct effect of situations and individual differences pales in comparison to the magnitude of interactions. In this light, the controversy in psychology concerning the relative importance of personality and situations assumes less importance in face of data that demonstrate that political participation is specific to the number of predictors, and multiply determined by them all.[6]

Rudolf Moos also suggests that cognitive sensitivity moderates the impact of situations on human behavior. He investigated the influence of setting and individual differences on the behavior of patients and staff in a psychiatric inpatient ward. Patients were typically social isolates, dependent, and immature. Presumably the

TABLE 6.3

Variance in Decision to Participate by National Situations, Situational Efficacy, General Efficacy, Past Influence of Self in Similar Situations and Past Influence of Others in Similar Situations

		Percent Variance
A	GPE	0
B	Situations	5
C	SE	0
D	Past Influence of others	0
E	Past Influence of self	1
A x B x C		1
A x B x D		2
A x B x E		1
B x C x D		3
B x C x E		2
B x D x E		6
A x B x C x D		8
A x B x C x E		12
A x B x D x E		12
A x C x D x E		4
B x C x D x E		12
A x B x C x D x E		9
Error		22
Total variance explained		78
N = 939		

	Situations	Past Influence of Self	Past Influence of Others	SE	GPE
Direct	5	1	0	0	0
Interaction	68	58	56	51	49
	73	59	56	51	49

TABLE 6.4

Variance in Decision to Participate by City Situations, Situational Efficacy, General Efficacy, Past Influence of Self in Similar Situations and Past Influence of Others in Similar Situations

		Percent Variance
A	GPE	0
B	Situations	7
C	SE	0
D	Past influence of others	0
E	Past influence of self	2
A x B x C		2
A x B x D		2
A x B x E		1
B x C x D		7
B x C x E		2
B x D x E		7
A x B x C x D		8
A x B x C x E		6
A x B x D x E		7
A x C x D x E		2
B x C x D x E		8
A x B x C x D x E		9
Error		30
Total variance explained		70

N = 793

	Situations	Past Influence of Others	Past Influence of Self	SE	GPE
Direct	7	0	2	0	0
Interaction	58	49	41	43	36
	65	49	43	43	36

TABLE 6.5

Variance in Decision to Participate by University Situations, Situational Efficacy, General Efficacy, Past Influence of Self in Similar Situations and Past Influence of Others in Similar Situations

		Percent Variance
A	GPE	0
B	Situations	3
C	SE	0
D	Past influence of others	0
E	Past influence of self	0
B x C		2
B x D		5
A x B x C		4
A x B x D		2
A x B x E		1
A x C x D		2
B x C x D		9
B x C x E		5
B x D x E		2
A x B x C x D		11
A x B x C x E		11
A x B x D x E		2
A x C x D x E		1
B x C x D x E		12
A x B x C x D x E		9
Error		19
Total variance explained		81
N = 705		

	Situations	SE	Past Influence of Others	Past Influence of Self	GPE
Direct	3	0	0	0	0
Interaction	75	66	55	43	43
	78	66	55	43	43

TABLE 6.6

Variance in Decision to Participate Explained by National Situations, Situational Efficacy, General Efficacy, Prior Situational Participation of Self, Past Influence of Others in Similar Situations

		Percent Variance
A	GPE	0
B	Situations	6
C	SE	2
D	Past influence of others	3
E	Past participation of self	25
A x B x C xE		1
B x C x D x E		4
A x B x C x D x E		6
Error		53
Total variance explained		47
N = 1840		

	Past participation of self	Situations	Past Influence of Others	SE	GPE
Direct	25	6	3	2	0
Interaction	11	11	10	11	7
	36	17	13	13	7

staff might be expected to be more discriminating. This was borne out, as settings "... did not elicit consistently different reactions from patients..." while context generally accounted for more staff behavior than psychological dispositions.[7]

While there were no extreme social isolates in this sample of young adults, the least cognitively sensitized people would be those who had little or no past political experience. Tables 6.6-8 include the entire sample, the majority of whom have not personally participated in similar political situations. This group is apt to be least discriminating. Although interactions are still important in Tables 6.6-8, in comparison with the more experienced group (Tables 3-5) this subpopulation's reduced ability to discriminate is reflected in the (1) expanded influence of primary effects* at the expense of interaction (particularly at the national level), (2) reduced variance associated with situational stimuli, and (3) reduced variance explained by the whole model.

What would happen if we could again select out a more discriminating sector among this enlarged population? Would the increased cognitive awareness again heighten the predictive power of the model? Would the behavior of the discriminating person once again be multiply determined largely by interactions?

One of the objectives of the multiple pretests was to isolate issues which were central to this population. Most of the students were interested in and had discussed the issues finally selected. Other questions were also asked about their interest in politics and election campaigns at each level of government. Combining the eight issue and interest questions, we constructed a political centrality index for each level of government. Each index was heavily skewed in the high centrality direction. Selecting only the top 45 percent (highest two scores) on the national centrality scale assured us of a politicized and aware subsample.

We compared this politicized group (Table 6.9) with the national case (Table 6.6) from the total population. The results are quite different. Past participation (Table 6.9) still has the largest direct influence, although the total main effect (7 percent) is again overshadowed by interactions (71 percent). The variance explained in this most concerned group is 31 percent larger than that for the whole population in Table 6.6. Situations again contribute to every significant interaction and are associated with more variance than the other predictors.

---

*Past situational participation of self (E) is now dichotomized between those who have and those who have not participated in a similar situation.

TABLE 6.7

Variance in Decision to Participate by City Situations, Situational Efficacy, General Efficacy, Prior Situational Participation of Self, Past Influence of Others in Similar Situations

		Percent Variance
A	GPE	0
B	Situations	4
C	SE	1
D	Past influence of others	1
E	Past participation of self	14
A x B x D x E		9
A x B x C x D		5
A x B x C x E		6
B x C x D x E		8
A x B x C x D x E		17
Error		35
Total variance explained		65
N = 1629		

	Past Participation of Self	Situations	Past Influence of Others	SE	GPE
Direct	14	4	1	1	0
Interaction	40	45	39	34	37
	54	49	40	35	37

TABLE 6.8

Variance in Decision to Participate by University Situations, Situational Efficacy, General Efficacy, Prior Situational Participation of Self, Past Influence of Others in Similar Situations

		Percent Variance
A	GPE	0
B	Situations	7
C	SE	0
D	Past influence of others	0
E	Past participation of self	11
B x C x D		1
B x C x E		2
B x D x E		6
A x B x C x D		6
A x B x C x E		2
A x B x D x E		3
B x C x D x E		2
A x B x C x D x E		13
Error		47
Total variance explained		53
N = 1570		

	Past Participation of Self	Situations	Past Influence of Others	SE	GPE
Direct	11	7	0	0	0
Interaction	34	35	31	26	24
	45	42	31	26	24

TABLE 6.9

Variance in Decision to Participate by National Situations, Situational Efficacy, General Efficacy, Past Influence of Others in Similar Situations, and Prior Situational Participation of Self Among Those for Whom the Issues and Politics Are Most Central[a]

		Percent Variance
A	GPE	0
B	Situations	1
C	SE	0
D	Past influence of others	1
E	Past participation of self	5
A x B x C		10
A x B x D		2
B x C x D		5
B x C x E		6
A x B x D x E		11
A x B x C x D		8
A x B x C x E		15
B x C x D x E		10
A x B x C x D x E		4
Error		22
Total variance explained		78
N = 887		

	Situations	SE	Past Participation of Self	GPE	Past Influence of Others
Direct	1	0	5	0	1
Interaction	71	58	46	50	40
	72	58	51	50	41

[a] Scores 8 and 9 on a 17-point politics and issue centrality scale.

The number of cases within the two highest centrality codes at the city and university levels is too low to continue to test, with any confidence, our thesis with the five predictors.* Yet we have seen two examples of the effect of increasing the discriminatory power of the population. We examined both those who had been sensitized by past situational participation, and the people for whom the issues and politics were most central. In both cases behavior was relatively specific to a number of predictors and multiply determined by all of them. The interactions which dominated the analysis strongly suggest an underlying cognitive process. The remarkable discriminative facility of the more politicized sector of the population also suggests limits to the proposition that global dispositions like general efficacy render situational stimuli equivalent.

Relative Contribution of Predictors:

The predictive power of models which include situational stimuli, prior learning, SE and psychodynamic dispositions is quite high. Moreover, these dispositions and beliefs are associated with interactions which explain a considerable amount of the variance in the decision to participate. For example, GPE contributes to interactions which explain 43, 36 and 49 percent of the variance in political participation at the university, city and national level, respectively (Tables 6.3-5).

What would happen if situations (or GPE) were removed from the five-predictor model? Earlier analysis suggests that situations are a necessary constituent to the interactions. Prior learning and situational efficacy effect the decision to participate in conjunction with characteristics of the immediate context. Remove the context and you destroy the base for much of the interaction. This should be particularly true among the more discriminating population.

Tables 6.3-5 show the impact of the five predictors among the cognitively sensitive, those who had experienced the situations before. Rerunning these tables without the situation variable emasculates the model. At the national level, explained variance plummets from 78 to 3 percent for the remaining four predictors. There is a corresponding drop at the city and university level. Clearly situations are an essential ingredient in the decision to participate. The second most important group of predictors is prior learning (E and D). Dropping SE brings a significant but smaller reduction in variance (20, 0, and 23 percent at the national, city and university level). Yet a reduction of 20 and 23 percent in explained variance associated

---

*The patterns were similar, however.

with the omission of SE at the university and national levels would be a significant weakening of the model.

Omitting GPE has the least effect in the university (8 percent) and city (0). The decrease in variance at the national level is slightly higher (12). The more marginal effect of omitting GPE, then, suggests that the earlier statement that "GPE contributes to interactions which explain 43, 36 and 49 percent of the variance" in political participation (Tables 6.3-5) is too expansive. Although GPE does not render situational stimuli equivalent or contribute to the decision to participate at a level that would satisfy a personality explanation of behavior, the increment in explained variance* from this global predictor is certainly large enough to warrant the continued use of GPE.

MULTIPLE CRITERION OF BEHAVIOR AND OTHER CAVEATS

If we set aside the notion that GPE is a personality disposition with its allied assumptions, we are still left with a global predictor which is associated with 8-12 percent of the variance in the interaction analysis. If this global sign represents the accumulated experience of the individual which rests relatively deep within the funnel of causality,[8] it is not surprising that it would be a weaker predictor of decisions to participate in a single setting than proximal variables such as situations and SE which are closer to the tip of the funnel. There could be, however, an overall configuration of behavior across the fifteen situations which is reflected in the general efficacy scale. Fishbein and Ajzen make this argument in their attempt to bolster the magnitude of the relationships between traditional measures of attitudes and specific behavior.[9]

To test this hypothesis we constructed an index of participation which included the fifteen situations. Those who consistently chose to participate in each situation were at one end, and those who always declined to participate were at the other. Presumably this clustering of behavior could be due to the respondent's general political efficacy. This notion was not sustained by the data. Crossing

---

*In the larger population where most have not been sensitized by prior situation participation (Tables 6.6-8), the loss in explained variance caused by eliminating general efficacy is 6, 15, and 12 percent at the national, city, and university level respectively. The total variance explained by the five factors is reduced in this population. However, dropping situations (or past participation) still has the largest relative impact on total variance. But in absolute terms, the effect is less than for the more discriminatory population examined in Tables 6.3-5. Excluding situations reduces total explained variance by 17, 35, and 36 percent at the national, city and university levels.

the participation index with the GPE scale shows the two measures are weakly related (Gamma = .10). General political efficacy accounts for one percent of the variance in the situational participation index (one-way analysis of variance). Thus the direct effect of GPE is not large when predicting participation in a specific situation or the overall configuration of participation.

Unstructured Situations:

There is another way one might strengthen the relationship between GPE and situational participation. Global dispositions may lead to participation when the actor has reliable expectations of the situation. To the extent that the situation is in flux, unstructured, relatively few cues are present, a person will have difficulty in knowing the appropriate role to play. Irving Crespi makes this argument as he says

> that in loosely structured situations, such as occur when crowds gather and in time of rapid social change, pre-existing attitudes are far less determining of behavior than the dynamics of the situation itself.[10]

If, as he suggests, voting is more structured than demonstrating, the relative influence of GPE should be greater on voting. On the other hand, social scientists have argued perhaps more often that it is the less routinized situation where personality has its freest reign.

We looked at the proportion of explained variance associated with GPE in demonstrations and voting situations. As one can see below, there is little evidence that dispositions were more important in explaining the voting act than demonstrating. At the university there is no difference. In national politics there is a modest gap, but in the opposite direction. It is only in city politics that there is a significant difference in the predicted direction.

Proportion of the Total Explained Variance
in the Decision to Demonstrate or Vote
Associated with GPE

	Demonstration	Vote
National	.19	.07
City	.03	.55
University	.64	.64

Structure exists not only in the objective character of the situation but also in the meaning that the actor gives to the setting. A new situation should appear more "structured" to someone who has participated before in an analogous context. This person should have a firmer grasp of his role and the expected cues which will emanate. Comparing the total sample with the smaller group of people who participated before in comparable settings will give us some purchase on the impact of subjective structure. As shown below, GPE is associated with relatively more variance among the population most likely to impart structure to the new situation. At least it is true in national and university politics. In the city there is a modest reversal.

Proportion of the Total Explained Variance
in the Decision to Participate
Associated with GPE[a]

	Those with Past Experience	Total Sample
National	.63	.15
City	.51	.57
University	.53	.45

[a]The proportions were derived from Tables 6.3-5, 8.

These figures, however, must be placed in the context of our earlier discussion of Tables 6.3-5, 8. First, GPE is associated with more variance among those with past experience, but so are the other four predictors in the model. Second, dropping GPE from the model among those most likely to impart subjective structure, reduces explained variance in the decision to participate less than does removing either of the other four predictors.

WITHIN SITUATIONS

Having examined the multiple effect of the five predictors, we now turn to the influence of GPE, SE, and prior learning on participation in *each* of the fifteen situations. Bowers suggests that observing a person's behavior across situations obscures the effect of individual differences. Holding situations constant is likely to magnify the effects of psychological dispositions.[11] This is similar to the "desert island" argument. If one were marooned on a desert island it is presumed that situational differences would be relatively narrow.* Thus a measure of GPE would be quite handy in understanding participation. Presumably measures of past experience and situational efficacy would also provide useful information.

Examining each of the fifteen situations reveals no startling revelations or new patterns (See, for example, Table 6.10). Removing the situation variable (but not the situation) predictably lowers the total variance explained; yet in some contexts it is still on the order of 30 to 40 percent.[12] Stimulus and response generalization best explains the decision to participate within situations. That is, the most parsimonious and powerful predictor is simply whether one participated in a comparable situation in the past. Generalization from this personal learning experience is the most influential variable in eleven of the fifteen situations. Moreover, past learning is a necessary constituent of all the larger interactions. Although with the situational variable removed, the amount of interaction is reduced throughout.

Situation efficacy and vicarious learning through the experience of others are roughly tied for second place across the different environments. SE has a very slight edge in national politics while this minimal difference is reversed at the city and university level. Neither variable is very directly related to participation; the largest primary effects are with petitioning and letter writing at the national level. (Table 6.10). In the other twelve situations the variance directly accounted for by either predictor is between 0 and 3 percent. Their major influence is through interaction with each other and personal past experience.

Our earlier observations of people's behavior *across* situations did not obscure the effect of individual differences. At least, the influence of GPE was not augmented by this intra-situation analysis and remained one of the weaker predictors.

MODERATOR VARIABLES

There are a number of other variables that could influence the cognitive process that appears to underly decisions to participate. Age, sex and perceived priorities are just a few of these.

---

*This, of course, depends on the perceptions of the castaway. As we saw in Chapter 4, people may place themselves in different situations mentally as well as experiencing them physically.

TABLE 6.10

Variance in Decisions to Participate by General Efficacy, Situational Efficacy, Past Influence of Others in Similar Situations and Prior Situational Participation of Self in National Situations

	Demonstrations %		Campaigns %		Vote %
A GPE	0		0		0
C SE	0		2		2
D Past influence of others	1		2		1
E Past participation of self	15		19		15
A x C x E	5	A x D 1	A x D	1
A x C x D	2	A x D x E 1	C x E	10
C x D x E	13		AxCxE	1
Error	64		75		70
Total variance explained	36		25		30
N =	421		404		429

	Petition %	Letter %
A GPE	0	0
C SE	1	7
D Past influence of others	5	8
E Past participation of self	5	11
C x D	1	D x E 1
A x C x D	1	
Error	87	73
Total variance explained	13	27
N =	275	311

Aging can affect political behavior in two ways. First, biological aging is associated with cognitive ability. Both the very old and the very young have retarded cognitive capacity. If sufficient numbers of either group were to participate in politics, the five factor model should predict less of their behavior and include fewer interactions. Age is also experientally related to political behavior. Between the elderly and the cognitively immature, aging is associated with increased political experience.[13] This should augment a person's discriminatory capacity and the power of the model to predict his behavior.

Sex:

It is frequently assumed that women are more susceptible to social stimuli than are men. Endler and Hunt found modest confirmation for this as situations contributed more to the anxious and hostile behavior of women than of men.[14]

We reran the five-factor model for both men and women, paying particular attention to the proportion of the total variance in the decision to participate that was associated with situational stimuli and the experience of others. Contrary to expectations, males are more sensitive to context than females, although the differences are modest (Table 6.11, Column A). Possibly females are more susceptible to the opinions and experience of others. Although the sign is right, it is only at the national level that women are really more affected than men by the experience of others. Again, the difference is small, not rising above 13 percent (Table 6.11, B).

Participating in similar situations in the past sharpens both male's and female's cognitive sensitivity to the nuances of the current situation. The modest differences that existed in Column A between the sexes are reduced even further among the more politicized respondents in Column D.

Unlike females who have had meager political experience, women whose political sensitivity has been sharpened by past activity are less likely to be swayed by the opinions of others. Rather, they are more inclined to be guided by their own past experiences and the interactions of that experience with their perceptions of the current situation.

Among this smaller but cognitively sensitive population, women actually follow the opinions of others in national and city politics less than do men (Table 6.11, E). "Others" are more important for females at the university (15 percent difference).

To sum up, the differences between the sexes are generally small.

TABLE 6.11

Difference Between Men and Women in the Proportion of the Total Explained Variance in the Decision to Participate Associated With Either Situations, Awareness of the Past Influence of Others or Situational Efficacy

	Total Sample		
	A Situations	B Others	C SE
National	-.06[a]	+.13	+.06
City	-.10	+.01	-.05
University	-.05	+.03	-.05

	Those Who Have Participated in Similar Situations Before		
	D Situations	E Others	F SE
National	-.08	-.03	-.03
City	+.03	-.11	+.03
University	0	+.15	+.05

[a]Minus (-) indicates that the variance explained by the predictor for males is greater than that for females. Thus -.06 means that six percent more variance in the decision to participate is associated with situations for males than for females.

There is scant evidence here that women are more likely to be led by the context of political participation than are men. Indeed, there is some movement in the opposite direction. Nor do the opinions of others appear to have a significantly greater hold on a woman's decision to participate.

Another hypothesis engages the traditional image of women. Are males more likely to rationally calculate their influence in a situation while women are swayed by less "logical" factors? Does the bias in early socialization experience and in the educational process which allegedly shunts young women away from mathematics, science and logical analysis, spill over into the political arena? If this is the case, then it is possible that the proportion of the total variance in the decision to participate that is associated with the calculation of situational efficacy could be less for females than for males. This hypothesis finds no comfort in the data. Neither in the total sample nor among those who have participated before is there a significant difference between the sexes in their propensity to calculate their political advantage in the various settings (Table 6.11, C and F).

Priorities and "Rational" Decisions:

The view that a person's decision to participate is based on his calculation that he can have some impact (SE) is very much a rational decision model. We saw that the product of this calculus of influence (SE) varied from situation to situation and was associated, on the average, with 20 percent of the variance in the decision to participate. This is not altogether surprising. People may make a quick calculus of their possible influence in a potential action setting without influence itself being the priority consideration in deciding whether to participate. For example, some situational stimuli may remind us of disastrous past experiences and shape negative expectations. Yet pushed by peers or other pressures of the situation we decide to participate (B—F). Similarly, we may believe that past efforts had little impact on government authorities. Thus, on encountering an analogous situation, we are not sanguine about our potential influence. However, we did have fun when we participated before and this looks like another good time (BxE—F).

After each respondent had made his participation decision, we asked him "why?" he made that decision. A single open-ended question touches only a portion of the cognitive activity underlying the decision. Yet the variety of responses do serve as examples of the fact that while practically everyone had tried to calculate influence in the situation, the primary reason they perceived for their decision varied considerably.*

---

*We assume that the first response given to the "Why?" did you make that participation decision, represents the primary reason they perceived for their action.

TABLE 6.12

First Reason Given by People for Their Participation Decision

	Influence[a]	Citizen Responsibility	Other
National demonstration	46%	7%	47%
University letter	43	4	53
City letter	40	5	55
National letter	39	5	56
National campaign	39	8	52
City demonstration	34	11	55
University demonstration	32	10	58
City vote	32	34	34
City campaign	31	5	64
National petition	31	2	67
University campaign	30	3	67
University petition	26	5	69
National vote	26	35	29
University vote	25	10	65
City petition	21	4	75

[a]Those who answered that their ability to influence or their lack of influence was the reason why they made their decision about whether to participate.

Some respondents said they would campaign, for example, because they knew the candidate. This reason was given mostly at the city and university level. Others said they would act because they wanted to express their opinion, no matter whether it was heard or not. Some responded that the activity sounded like fun (demonstration in Washington, D.C.)! There were other people who felt they had to act because it was required of them as responsible citizens. This response was most typical in city and national voting (Table 6.12). Others said they made their decision because they believed that the situation had (or had not) afforded them the opportunity to influence the political authority in question. A rational-decision explanation should be a better predictor of the decision to participate among this last group.

To test this hypothesis, we controlled for people's perceptions of why they made their participation decision in each of the fifteen situations. MANOVA was used to examine the effect of SE, GPE and past participation experience of self on the decision to participate.*

There are a number of differences between those who gave other reasons and those who mentioned influence. First, in thirteen of the fifteen situations, the deductive process leading through SE explains a larger amount of the variance in the decision to participate among people who see the exercise of influence as the primary reason for their action.

When influence is not their chief consideration (even though they may calculate it), the impact of SE drops.** Second, the total explained variance in the three-factor model increases sharply among those who are concerned about their influence. A prime contributor to the increase is the interaction between SE and one's past participation experience. Finally, the relative power of SE compared to GPE is greater when influence is perceived to be the major consideration in the decision. This concern with influence is apparently situation specific, and it does not augment the relative impact of GPE.

Only in city and national voting situations did significant numbers of people infer they acted out of a sense of citizen responsibility. Yet even among this group, SE is associated with most of the explained variance. Apparently members of the attentive public who see voting as a negative or positive means to fulfill their citizenship obligations also calculate the influence the act will have upon politics (see Table 6.13).

Table 6.13 shows the importance of knowing the ordering of situation related perceptions. As we move away from "other" reasons for participation to citizenship responsibility and influence priorities, the variance in the decision to participate associated with SE increases by as much as 75 and 66 percent at the city and national level. Differences between those who cite influence or other reasons are not always so large. Yet this is a consistent trend in every setting, with the exception of writing letters to national politicians and participating in university demonstrations.

---

*A smaller number of cases are available for within situation analysis. This N was further reduced by the controls. Therefore, one predictor variable, past influence of others, was eliminated from the MANOVA analysis.

**Actually, as we shall see, it is only when "other" reasons are given for the decision that the impact of SE drops significantly. Situational efficacy continues to be important among those who cite citizen responsibility as the reason for their action.

TABLE 6.13

Variance in the Decision to Vote by General Efficacy, Situational Efficacy and Prior Situational Participation of Self Among Those Who Gave Either Influence, Citizenship Responsibility or Other Reasons for Their Decision

City Vote

		Influence	Citizen Responsibility		Other
A	GPE	0	0		0
C	SE	0	0		4
E	Past participation of self	0	0		9
A x C		17	2	A x E	5
C x E		60	40		
A x C x E		2	35		
Error		21	23		82
Total variance explained		79	77		18
Variance associated with SE		79	77		4
N =		160	170		170

National Vote

		Influence	Citizen Responsibility		Other
A	GPE	0	0		5
C	SE	0	0		8
E	Past participation of Self	0	0		30
A x C		1	10	A x E	6
C x E		44	69		4
A x C x E		30	1		2
Error		25	20		40
Total variance explained		75	80		55
Variance associated with SE		75	80		14
N =		130	175		145

Clearly, cognitive activity which links a situation to past experience, or calculates one's potential for influencing public officials, is significant to the explanation of why members of the attentive public participate in politics. Beyond this, those aspects of the situation which are perceived as most salient to the individual appear to moderate the relationships and suggest limits to the power of a rational decision model involving situational efficacy.

FOOTNOTES AND REFERENCES

[1] The response categories to the situational participation question were: Yes, yes probably, probably not, no, unsure. Those who indicated they were "unsure" were dropped from the subsequent analysis.

[2] Alan Liska, "Emergent Issues in the Attitude-Behavior Consistency Controversy," *American Sociological Review* 39 (April, 1974), 262. Also see C. R. Tittle and R. J. Hill, "The Accuracy of Self Reported Data and Prediction of Political Activity," *Public Opinion Quarterly* 31 (Spring, 1967), 103-106.

[3] Generalization from past situations should have an important effect on one's behavior in current but similar situations. But many have had no past experience in a *similar* situation. On the other hand, they may have used other strategies, and it is possible that this situational experience could spill over into the current setting. To test this notion, we constructed a summary index of past situational participation (PPI) for each individual. The additive index indicated the number of times in the past each person had participated in one of the fifteen situations. This index was included in the AID analysis with the other predictors. Contrary to expectations, there was little "spillover." PPI was somewhere in the roots of the explanatory tree, accounting for less than one percent of the variance in participation. People appeared to be very discriminating as past situation experience in *similar* situations continued to be an important predictor. Therefore, PPI was dropped from the subsequent analysis.

The impressive discriminatory power of people has frequently been treated as measurement error or behavioral inconsistency. See William Mischel, "Toward a Cognitive Social Learning Reconceptualization of Personality," *Psychological Review* 80 (July, 1973), p. 258.

[4] Mischel, *op. cit.*, 1973, 256, 258.

⁵ As mentioned earlier, there have been a small number of studies in psychology over the last ten years which have examined the main effect as well as the variance accounted for by the interaction of psychodynamic signs (anxiety, hostility, sociability, etc.) and situations. These investigations are usually restricted to two or three predictors. Prior learning and situation specific beliefs (for example, SE) are not included.

By and large these studies show that the direct effect of individual differences and situations is less than the variance accounted for by their interaction.

See M. Argyle and B. Little, "Do Personality Traits Apply to Social Behavior?," *Journal of Theory of Social Behavior* 2 (1972), 1-35; N. Endler and J.McV. Hunt, "Sources of Behavioral Variance as Measured by the S-R Inventory of Anxiousness," *Psychological Bulletin* 65 (June, 1966), 336-346; Endler and Hunt, "S-R Inventories of Hostility and Comparisons of the Proportions of Variance from Persons, Responses, and Situations for Hostility and Anxiousness," *Journal of Personality and Social Psychology* 9 (August, 1968), 309-315; Endler and Hunt, "Generalizability of Contributions from Sources of Variance in the S-R Inventories of Anxiousness," *Journal of Personality* 37 (March, 1969), 1-24; and Rudolf Moos, "Situational Analysis of a Therapeutic Community Milieu," *Journal of Abnormal Psychology* 73 (February, 1968), 49-61. For research on interactions between attitudes and social support in predicting behavior see William J. Bowers, "Normative Constraints on Deviant Behavior in the College Context," *Sociometry* 31 (December, 1968), 370-385.

⁶ Some psychologists engaged in research on situations speak of behavior being "idiosyncratically" organized for each individual. Neither in this study nor in the research designs commonly employed in "situation" analysis in Psychology can we exclude the possibility that behavior is organized personally at a higher level. Here we have seen for example that people with certain types of behavioral histories which include past success in influence attempts or political experience react differently in situations than do others.

⁷ Rudolf H. Moos, *op. cit.*, 51, 56, 59.

⁸ Angus Campbell, Philip Converse, Warren Miller, and Donald Stokes, *The American Voter* (New York: John Wiley, 1960), Chapter 2.

⁹ Martin Fishbein and Icek Ajzen, "Attitudes Towards Objects as Predictors of Single and Multiple Behavioral Criteria," *Psychological Review* 81 (January, 1974), 59-74.

¹⁰ Irving Crespi, "What Kinds of Attitude Measures are Predictive of Behavior?," *Public Opinion Quarterly* 35 (Fall, 1971), 334.

[11] Kenneth Bowers, "Situationism in Psychology: An Analysis and Critique," *Psychological Review* 80 (September, 1973), 324.

[12] Total variance explained by GPE, SE, past influence of others, and past participation of self in each situation.

	Average variance explained by strategy across three levels	University	City	National
Sit-in	33%	31%	31%	36%
Vote	34	28	45	30
Campaign	33	41	33	25
Petition	24	17	41	13
Letter	21	14	21	27

[13] Verba and Nie demonstrate that with controls for length of residence and social economic status, there is a gradual increase in voting throughout the life cycle that continues past the age 65. Overall participation in politics does decline slightly after age 65, but not the sharp drop usually associated with the later years. Sidney Verba and Norman Nie, *Participation in America: Political Democracy and Social Equality* (New York: Harper and Row, 1972), Chapter 9.

[14] Endler and Hunt, 1968, *op. cit.*, 314.

Chapter 7

SUMMARY AND CONCLUSIONS

We have selected a limited set of parameters from the host of factors which social scientists have linked to political behavior. This does not mean that the others do not contribute to the decision to participate. Rather, the variables in this analysis were included in a self-conscious attempt to suggest the theoretical implications and empirical limits of some of the assumptions we bring to the question of why people participate in politics.

PSYCHODYNAMIC

Figure 1.1 in Chapter 1 incorporates a number of influence and learning models. One set of assumptions traces the antecedents of political participation through a psychodynamic process. Early learning in the family of origin (G) creates stable personality or attitudinal dispositions such as political efficacy (A). These psychological patterns formed in childhood pass relatively unchanged into adulthood. By rendering situational stimuli equivalent, this global dispo-

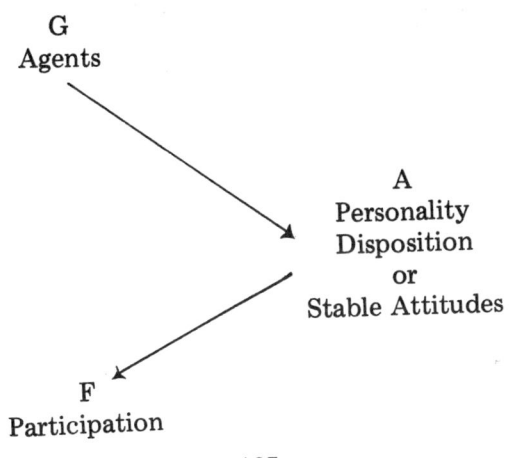

sition causes the adult to behave in a consistent and predictable manner (F).

There are four points where the psychodynamic model must be corroborated. First, the family should be the prime socialization source for political efficacy (G-A). Second, one's sense of political efficacy should be relatively stable across the life cycle. Third, personality dispositions or global attitudes like efficacy should not vary significantly across situations. And, finally, such dispositions must cause people to participate in politics in a predictable manner (A-F).

Taking the early learning assumption first, we found little support in Chapters 2 and 3 for familial primacy. The socialization role of the family appears to change as countries undergo socioeconomic transformation. The dominant influence of the family is replaced by the secondary school and job in later stages of national development. Nor does political efficacy seem to be stable across the life cycle. Other studies have noted the mean and individual changes in efficacy levels between 1952 and 1973 in the United States. We found that participatory job environments could take workers who had acquired a low or medium sense of efficacy earlier in life and move them into the higher reaches of political confidence.

Is political efficacy a personality disposition? Personality traits are presumed to endure across time and to be relatively stable from one situation to the next. Political efficacy responds to life cycle changes and is not generalizable across situations, at least not at a level that would satisfy a personality theorist. The average cross-situational correlations between efficacy scores is .32. Thus there is real question whether we can continue to treat political efficacy as a global psychological disposition or personality attribute. Its variation across situations leads us to think otherwise. The same question can, of course, be asked of other dispositions or attitudes that are treated as relatively stable in the literature. It is interesting in this regard that Jennings and Niemi found considerable openness to change among young and older adults in "personality characteristics" such as interpersonal trust, opinion strength, and self confidence. Their measures were more content-specific than some general and intensive measures of these dispositions which often serve to heighten consistency. Yet the highest over-time correlations for young adults (aged 17-18 years in 1965 and 25-26 in 1973) for the three dispositions was Tau beta .27. The dispositions of their parents (aged 40-54 in 1965 and 48-62 in 1973) were somewhat more consistent as the highest correlation was .42[1].

The weak support for the other assumptions of the psychodynamic model is joined by evidence that political efficacy is too limited a predictor to satisfy a personality explanation of political participation. That is, we found no evidence for the proposition that political efficacy has a "generalized causal effect" on political participation which leads people to behave consistently across situations. Thus the psychodynamic model provides us with limited guidance in our search for the antecedents of political participation.

Where does this leave the connection between the socialization agents and the decision of adults to participate? We demonstrated in Chapter 3 that the agents did have considerable impact upon one's sense of political confidence. What Chapters 5 and 6 suggested, however, was that the link between the agents and political participation is unlikely to be through political efficacy construed as a personality factor or a stable attitude. Instead, the connection, to the extent it exists, is through cognitive processes which we will summarize below.

SITUATIONS

Another path of influence comes *directly* from the situation. In stimulus-response parlance, the stimulus (situation) illicits a response (decision to participate).

$$B \qquad\qquad\qquad\qquad F$$
$$\text{Situation} \longrightarrow \text{Situational Participation}$$

Some "situationists" employ S-R designs and eschew the "mentalism" of the personality theorists. More generally, they consider personality, attitudes, and cognition to be superfluous to our understanding of behavior.

We looked at the direct relationship between situations and the decision to participate. Situations are associated with 19 percent of the variance in participation (Table 6.2) when GPE and SE are the only other predictors in the model. If one adds perceptions of past experience, situations never directly explain more than 7 percent of the variance (Tables 6.3-6.9). Context is important to the participation decision, but chiefly through interactions with the person's perception of the situation, and his perceptions of the past influence of himself and others.

The direct relation, then, between setting and political participation exists chiefly by default. When past experience and situational beliefs are added to the model, direct effect declines sharply and the situation's contribution to interactions soars.

RATIONAL DECISIONS TO PARTICIPATE

A broader focus than S-R relations is the citizen's calculation of influence. The assumption is that people decide to participate after calculating their advantage in each situation. This view emphasizes the role of situational efficacy and its interaction with situational characteristics and past experience in the decision process.

People generally do not have sufficient awareness of the issues or information about public officials to make a purely rational, means-ends decision. Instead, there is a calculation of influence akin to what Herbert Simon refers to as "satisficing." Let us assume that there is a public policy or issue that is of personal concern to the citizen. He is asked to join a petition drive. He looks at the characteristics of the situation (B): petition strategy, collective effort, nature of the public officials, and so on. He tries to calculate how likely it is that this act would influence those officials (C). What he has to go on, then, are his perceptions of the situation, the officials, and his own concern.

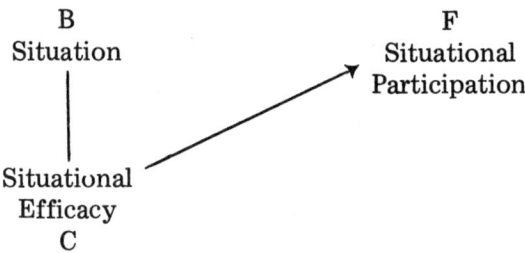

Depending on the nature of the situation, he will be more or less confident of his potential influence.

We saw in Chapter 5 that political confidence does vary considerably across situations. In the multivariate analysis, SE was associated with about 20 percent of the variance in participation. This is not an insignificant amount of variance, but it does place the SE-participation relation closer to the range of general political efficacy. It was found, however, that when we probe peoples' perceptions of the situations, influence is not always their first consideration. When it is, SE is associated with more than three quarters of the variance in the decision to participate. Much of this increase in explained variance comes through interactions with past experience. We shall now turn to this more comprehensive model.

COGNITIVE PROCESSING

Neither the assumptions of the psychodynamic, S-R, or rational decision approaches are by themselves adequate in the prediction or explanation of the decision to participate in politics. The direct influence of many of the predictors is limited. Yet we must be cautious about concluding that these weak *direct* relationships are due wholly to measurement error, inconsistent, or should we say unreliable, individuals, or theoretical errors in the selection of predictors.

The situation, situational beliefs (SE), one's own past experiences in similar settings, and what we think have been the experiences of others in these situations are all significant factors. What seems to be particularly important, however, is the statistical interaction and cognitive process that joins these variables.

True when we speak of cognition, we are referring to a psychological process that is rarely, if ever, directly observable.[2] We infer its existence from the relations between verbal, written or motor behavior we observe in others, and our own personal experience with "thinking." In this regard, social scientists have the same problem as high energy physicists, although on a grander scale. The physicist notes a relation between two observables. The relation can only be "explained" by the existence of a third particle, which his equipment is too insensitive to detect. The history of the physical sciences should give rise to guarded optimism as the development of more sensitive techniques frequently converted the unobservable link to the observable, with the characteristics that had been hypothesized.

The circumstantial evidence assembled in this study suggests that cognition is the theoretical glue that binds the parts of the model in Chapter 1. Cognition mediates between prior situational experience and the current situation, and the current situation and the decision to participate. This process does appear to share some characteristics with the stimulus-outcome contingencies used to explain animal learning. The respondents' decision to participate was shaped by their expectancy about outcomes which interacted with situational stimuli and past learning. That a cognitive process underlies this interaction model is further suggested by 1) the variation in interaction between the predictors and the predictive power of the model with the cognitive (past) learning experience of the population, and 2) the dramatic variation in the predictive power of interactions between SE and past experience with individual differences in perceptions of the priorities in each situation.

There are many important areas here for future exploration. For example, what characteristics of situations elicit behavioral response? In the social sciences we are very much at the early stage of discovering the impact of situations and their interaction with other predictors. The construction of taxonomies of situations awaits both the replication and amplification of these studies. But if we are interested in explanation and theory building, we must probe the cognitive processes involved. How, for example, does cognition structure the meaning we give situations? Reality depends on one's methods of knowing it. Imagine different people looking at an object on the ground. Depending on his cognitive complexity and past anthropological experience, one person sees a peculiar looking rock, another a bone, another a fossil, another sees the fossil as the jaw fragment of an ancient proto-man, another finds evidence for the existence and structure of Australopithecus Africanus and the missing link.[3] Thus the stability in behavior we find across settings may have less to do with a stable attitude or personality than consistencies in cognitive organization.

Another question is: how do individuals associate situational stimuli with outcomes? One person sees a potential action situation as an opportunity to meet new people. Another sees an opportunity to exercise influence. Whether the situation involves an individual versus a collective strategy, then, has a different meaning for these two people. Their calculus will be guided by their own past experiences (or their perceptions of the experience of others) which they judge to be sufficiently similar to their perceptions of the current situation. Those personal factors which affect judgements about "similarity" are still generally unknown. Here the current situation may stimulate a cognitive search through past learning. One looks for cues, signposts to current action. Perceptions of past experience of self and others, situations, and SE all interact to influence the decision to participate. The fact that a person's cognitive activity and organization is so difficult to separate from what he perceives is why interactions have explained a substantial part of the variance in the decisions to participate. The nature of individual search activity, then, the cognitive structure and skills we bring to it, and the way we perceive and organize stimuli are all promising areas of future study.

A final comment concerning the relation between situations and outcomes and future research. Throughout this discussion we have suggested that situational characteristics stimulate a search and generalization of past experiences. It is also possible that one's perception or vision of the immediate situation may dominate or block other relevant stimuli. Posner, Nissen and Klein demonstrated that

Summary And Conclusions

visual stimuli often prevail over auditory and kinetic stimuli which emanate from the same situation. Demonstrations of visual dominance are not limited to these stimuli, however. Visual stimuli may also dominate memory.[4]

This has several important implications for our research. If we observe subjects in a natural setting, visual stimuli from the current situation may on occasion dominate their memory of past experience. This would reduce interaction and heighten the S-R characteristics of the learning process which underlie the decision to participate. Clearly, stimulus training, attention, and individual differences will determine the degree of visual dominance in any given situation.

SOCIALIZATION AGENTS

The review of these different approaches helps locate the place of the socialization agents in the decision to participate. You will remember that one possible line of influence is through psychodynamic processes. However, the variability of political confidence and the relatively weak relation between GPE and participation make this influence channel less probable. The other path to adult political participation is through the cognitive process which links the current situation, past experience in the socialization agent, and present calculations of influence (G x B x C→F, Figure 1.1).

Let us say we observe a citizen in a potential action setting. His past experiences affect his perception of the situation. The situation also acts as a stimulus; he begins to search his past experience for decision guides. Experiences in the family, school, and peer group are a subset of his total prior experiences. Some of these adventures may be remembered, others forgotten. And, unless we wish to slip back into the psychodynamic model, we must assume that the relevance of these prior experiences to the present situation will depend on our ability to remember them, and their similarity to the current setting.

Whether this prior learning is seen as relevant to the current situation, and therefore remembered, is an important area of future research. We would offer two general hypotheses in this regard. First, the association between participation in these agents and decisions to participate will be stronger in the attentive public than the less attentive.* Those who are more discriminating will see the

---

*Although, as we have seen, the relations with some agents may be stronger than with others, depending on the level of socioeconomic development of the society.

similarity between past and current environments. Second, although these relationships may be stronger among the attentive public, they still will be relatively weak (both directly and through interactions) when compared with the contribution of the other factors in Model 1.1. This can be partially explained by the fact that those who are politicized will have past experience in voting, letter writing, petitioning, demonstrating, and so on. This past experience is likely to appear more relevant to current setting than less directly related situations in the family.

EITHER PERSONALITY OR SITUATIONS?

The "either-or" debate over the relative importance of individual differences and situations does not rest easily with the results of this study.

Situations:

The strict situationalist,* who looks only to stimulus-response or operant learning models that relegate cognition and perception to the dustbin of "mentalism," will also be hard pressed by these data. He must face the impressive increment in explained variance that accompanies the addition to the situational model of the subject's perception of the past influence of himself and others and his belief that he can be influential (SE) in the immediate situation. These last variables are all "mental." That is, they are based on the personal cognition and perception of the subject.

Personality:

The classic psychoanalytic view that traits will render behavior constant from one situation to the next also finds little support, at least at the level that would reassure a personality theorist. Directly and through interactions, general political efficacy consistently accounts for the least variance in participation. Nor does GPE predict well the overall configuration of behavior.

We could argue, as psychologists have for other dispositions, that general political efficacy is a genotypic personality disposition. It endures even though its overt response forms (phenotypic behavior

---

*While some situationalists reject internal psychological states as explanations of behavior, they do not reject the individual in their analysis. Witness the emphasis on a person's past learning history in the stimulus-response paradigms in experimental psychology.

Summary And Conclusions

such as situational efficacy or situational participation) change. The problem with this theoretical construction is that it is not any more useful for predicting human political behavior, than it is for predicting appropriate therapeutic modifications of behavior in clinical psychology.

This argument should not be taken to mean that other psychological dispositions will not be important determinants of participation, any more than we mean to suggest that some situations will not be trivial indicators of political behavior. Ego strength, self esteem, internal-external control, need achievement, social trust, political trust and polictical cynicism may all be less limited in their explanation of participation. Of course, they might not. Does this mean that political confidence is not useful in understanding why people decide to participate in politics? No, it does not for a number of reasons. First, the "funnel of causality" was conceived in 1960 as a theoretical meeting ground for the controversy between sociologists and some election study people over the prediction of voting choice.[5] By the same token, it is not necessary here to accept the personality assumption about efficacy nor theoretically exclude it for its mentalistic pretensions. This study suggests that it can be conceived of as a cognitive belief which is reactive to situational stimuli and demonstrably important to the explanation of significant forms of political participation.

Second, to continue with the funnel of causality metaphor, GPE can be thought of as a constellation of cognitive beliefs derived from past experience, which causes some generalization of behavior across situations. That is, in predicting situational behavior, it is somewhere in the recesses of the funnel in contrast to proximal variables like SE and situations which are close to the tip of the funnel. Unfortunately, GPE did not predict any better an overall configuration of participation (Chapter 6) than it did situation specific behavior. It was, however, associated with 8-12 percent of the variance in participation. This "small" amount of variance should be embarrassing only to those adopting a personality explanation of behavior. Others, because of their desire for parsimony and/or their theoretical interest in metaphors such as the funnel of causality, will see this increment in explanation as certainly large enough to continue tagging GPE in the future.

Third, the sample in this study is of the attentive public. This can restrict the range of the efficacy responses which will depress the relationships between efficacy and participation below what one might expect to find in the general public. The general population is also less interested in politics; therefore political confidence may be more stable across situations.

Fourth, the selection of situations is an important determinant of the relative influence of situations and GPE on behavior. If one chooses voting situations with quite similar characteristics, the influence of situations compared to GPE will decline. This does not mean that GPE is likely to be more important in voting than in other activity, at least among the attentive public. In Chapter 6 the proportion of total explained variance associated with GPE was generally not greater for voting than for the demonstration decisions.

Fifth, if one widens the range of situations and behavior (political assassination?), underlying psychological tendencies may become more important. Endler and Hunt found that personal differences had greater impact on hostile than on anxious behavior.[6] Moos discovered that the individual differences of patients in a psychiatric hospital predicted well their smoking behavior, while settings accounted for more variance in talking.[7] In this analysis, however, the presence of GPE normally accounted for less than 12 percent of the variance in letter writing, demonstrations, campaigning, and voting behavior at all three levels of politics.

Finally, certain individual differences of people may affect the variability of efficacy across situations. Bem and Allen showed that selecting persons who self identify themselves beforehand as being variable or non-variable on a relevant psychological dimension, will increase the consistency across situations of the trait in question. In these terms, we could have asked the subjects: "how much do you vary from one situation to another in how politically confident you are?"[8] The intercorrelations between SE across fifteen settings should be higher among those who report they change very little. The correlations between GPE and SE should also increase. Whether the variance in political participation explained by GPE among this "stable" group would also be higher is problematical. Possibly one could ask the respondents how much they vary from one situation to another in their inclination to participate politically. If GPE explains more variance in participation among the stable group, then one has uncovered an important personal difference or moderator variable.

MODERATOR VARIABLES AND SOCIAL CLASS

In Chapter 6 we discussed the possible effect of sex and age on the results of this study. We also saw how education affected the influence of the agents. How might social stratification moderate the findings reported in previous chapters? Let us first consider three hypotheses with regard to GPE within the lower classes. First, GPE will be a better predictor of SE. Second, political confidence

TABLE 7.1

Correlation Between General Political Efficacy and Situational Efficacy Among the Most and Least Politicized

Politicization	National	City	University
Highest	.27	.30	.26
Lowest	.29	.26	.28

will be more stable across situations. Third, GPE will be a stronger predictor of the lower classes' decisions to participate than among the attentive public.

It has frequently been demonstrated in the literature that members of the lower classes have less experience with the types of participation on which we have focused. Thus to approximate these class differences we segregated the university sample into the least and most politicized groups. Contrary to expectations, the correlations between GPE and SE only modestly improve in national and university politics among the least politicized. The correlation is actually smaller among the least politicized in the city (Table 7.1).

Nor can we confirm the second hypothesis. Political confidence is not more stable across situations among the less politically concerned. Quite the contrary. Chapter 5 showed (Figures 5.2-4) that controls for past situational experience actually reduce variation in SE. Those who had participated in similar situations more typical of the higher classes and felt that they had been influential, are less variable in SE from one situation to the next. There is not much evidence for the third hypothesis either. GPE is associated with more variance in participation among that part of the sample with *more* political experience (Chapter 6). Moreover, the ratio of explained variance in participation associated with situations and GPE among the *most politicized* is lower (1.4 to 1, respectively) than among the least concerned (1.5 to 1). These differences sharpen at the national level if we turn from interest and informational measures of politicization to measures of past political participation.

We would like to summarize at this point the differences we found between the two strata, because they may be indicative of what we will find if we apply this design to the mass public. Among the lower strata:

1. There will, of course, be less political participation.
2. What past participation experience the mass public does have will be more directly tied to their decision to participate than for the more attentive social strata.
3. Their prior political experience will be chiefly with voting. Thus, current behavior will be dominated by the voting act.
4. GPE will continue to be the weakest predictor of the decision to participate. Although the distribution of efficacy responses will be broader, their impact on participation will be attenuated by the reduced cognitive sensitivity of the mass public.
5. Because of less cognitive sensitivity, there will be fewer predictable interactions among the variables. Interactions will also explain less of the variance in participation.
6. Situations will continue to be the best predictor of participation decisions. However, the *direct* impact of setting will be more important than its contribution to participation through interactions.

In this sense, the mass public is closer to true S-R mobilization in which context will move them directly to engage in "spontaneous" activity. The importance of situations in the general population is not without its strategic implications. Those who are concerned about the housing, health care, security, and participation of the lower classes will look to the immediate manipulation of situational environment. Psychodynamic approaches, by contrast, would treat the longterm intractability of low political confidence.

ORGANIZATIONAL SETTINGS AND POLITICAL EXPERIENCE

Much of what has been assumed here with regard to the low political participation, less cognitive sensitivity, and the reduced number of interactions among the mass public rests on a particular vision of what is political. We chose to focus on voting, campaigning, petitioning, contacting, and demonstrating because these were the types of political behavior most often mentioned in the pretests as being available to the American public. A review of the literature would also show that this type of participation is the focus for most of the research on mass political behavior in the United States. The limitation of political activity to these standard measures, however, does reduce the amount of variance in situational participation and past situational experience that we could realistically expect to find among the working class.

Summary And Conclusions 139

A political economist would widen this political spectrum appreciably. What goes on *within* the factories and offices is also real politics. Things that workers value are allocated authoritatively within the work organization with great regularity. Moreover, the work organization frequently causes the worker to do things he would prefer not to do. Both are standard definitions of *political* activity. The observation that it may be a more rational "political" act for the average worker to lobby his boss about a need than to vote in a national election, speaks to our sometimes limited construction of politics.

Few workers may write letters to their congressman or take an active part in an election campaign. Many, however, have at some time contacted their foreman to negotiate work roles or discuss grievances. Some workers may never have contacted a foreman, nor heard of others who had done so. Yet the conditions might be so intolerable that they were moved to action (B→F). Others may have contacted a foreman in the past, felt they were influential, and decided to try it again (E x B x C→F). The point we wish to make here is that the theoretical design used in this book could be applied to the mass public. We are limited only in the amount of variance that exists. If we choose to restrict our image of the "political," we will predictably find less interest, participation, cognitive sensitivity, and interaction. Stimulus-response and incremental learning will characterize this process. On the other hand, we can broaden our image of politics and move to political arenas more familiar to workers.* If we do this, we shall find more concern, information, past experience, situational participation, cognitive sensitivity and interaction.

---

*I am suggesting a more catholic view of politics here, not the abandonment of our concern with traditional political activity.

FOOTNOTES AND REFERENCES

[1] M. Kent Jennings and Richard Niemi, "The Persistence of Political Orientations: An Over-Time Analysis of Two Generations," *British Journal of Political Science* 8 (July, 1978), 336, 360-361.

[2] See M. L. Deflear and F. R. Westie, "Attitude as a Specific Concept," *Social Forces* 42 (October, 1963), 17-31; and footnote 15, Chapter 1 in this book.

[3] This example was liberally taken from Kenneth Bowers, "Situationism in Psychology: An Analysis and a Critique," *Psychological Review*, 80 (September, 1973), 331.

[4] Michael I. Posner, Mary Jo Nissen and Raymond M. Klein, "Visual Dominance: An Information-Processing Account of Its Origins and Significance," *Psychological Review* 83 (March, 1976), 157-171.

[5] Angus Campbell, Philip Converse, Warren Miller and Donald Stokes, *The American Voter* (New York: John Wiley, 1960), Chapter 2.

[6] Norman Endler and J. McV. Hunt, "S-R Inventories of Hostility and Comparisons of the Proportions of Variance from Persons, Responses, and Situations for Hostility and Anxiousness," *Journal of Personality and Social Psychology* 9 (August, 1968), 312-313.

[7] Rudolf Moos, "Sources of Variance in Responses to Questionnaires and in Behavior," *Journal of Abnormal Psychology* 74 (1969), 405-412.

[8] Daryl Bem and Andrea Allen, "On Predicting Some of the People Some of the Time: The Search for Cross-Situational Consistencies in Behavior," *Psychological Review* 81 (November, 1974), 512. An example of the type of question Bem and Allen used was "How much do you vary from one situation to another in how friendly and outgoing you are?" Responses were ranged on a seven point scale from "not at all" to "extremely."

BIBLIOGRAPHY

Aberbach, Joel. "Power Consciousness: A Comparative Analysis." *American Political Science Review*, 71 (December, 1977), 1544-1560.

_____ and Jack Walker. *Race in the City: Political Trust and Public Policy in the New Urban System.* Boston: Little, Brown, 1973.

Abramson, Paul. "Generational Change in American Electoral Behavior." *American Political Science Review*, 68 (March, 1974), 93-105.

_____. "Political Efficacy and Political trust among Black School Children: Two Explanations." *Journal of Politics*, 34 (November, 1972), 1243-1275.

_____. *The Political Socialization of Black Americans, A Critical Evaluation of Research on Efficacy and Trust.* New York: the Free Press, 1977.

Adinolfi, Allen A. "Relevance of Person Perception to Clinical Psychology." *Journal of Consulting and Clinical Psychology*, 37 (August, 1971), 167-176.

Ajzen, Icek. "Attitudinal vs. Normative Messages: An Investigation of Differential Effects of Persuasive Communications on Behavior." *Sociometry*, 34 (June, 1971), 263-280.

Ajzen, Icek and Martin Fishbein. "Attitudinal and Normative Variables as Predictors of Specific Behaviors." *Journal of Personality and Social Psychology*, 27 (July, 1973), 41-57.

_____. "The Prediction of Behavioral Intentions in a Choice Situation." *Journal of Experimental Social Psychology*, 5 (October, 1969), 400-416.

_____. "The Prediction of Behavior from Attitudinal and Normative Variables." *Journal of Experimental Social Psychology*, 6 (October, 1970), 466-487.

Albrecht, Stan and Kerry Carpenter. "Attitudes as Predictors of Behavior Versus Behavior Intentions: A Convergence of Research Traditions." *Sociometry*, 39 (March, 1976), 1-10.

Alker, Henry. "Is Personality Situationally Specific or Intrapsychically Consistent." *Journal of Personality*, 40 (1972), 1-16.

Allen, Vernon. "Situational Factors in Conformity," in Leonard Berkowitz (ed.), *Advances in Experimental Social Psychology*, Volume 2. New York: Academic Press, 1965.

Allport, Gordon and Henry Odbert. "Trait Names: A Psycholexical Study," *Psychological Monographs*, 47 (1936), entire issue.

Almond, Gabriel and Sidney Verba. *The Civic Culture*. Princeton: Princeton University Press, 1963.

Andersen, Kristi. "Working Women and Political Participation, 1952-1972." *American Journal of Political Science*, 19 (August, 1975), 439-454.

Anderson, Clifford and Betty Nesvold. "A Skinnerian Analysis of Conflict Behavior: Waldon II Goes Cross National," *American Behavioral Scientist*, 15 (July-August, 1972), 883-909.

Anderson, N. H. and A.A. Barrios. "Primacy Effects in Personality Impression Formation." *Journal of Abnormal and Social Psychology*, 69 (1961), 35-40.

Arbuthnot, Jack. "Sex, Sex-role Identity, and Cognitive Style." *Perceptual and Motor Skills*, 41 (October, 1975), 435-440.

Argyle, M. and B. Little. "Do Personality Traits Apply to Social Behavior?" *Journal of Theory of Social Behavior*, 2 (1972), 1-35.

Aries, Philippe. *Centuries of Childhood*. New York: Knopf, 1962.

Arrington, Theodore. "Some Effects of Political Experience on Issue Consciousness and Issue Partisanship Among Tuscon Party Activists." *American Journal of Political Science*, 19 (November, 1975), 695-702.

Arterton, F. Christopher. "The Impact of Watergate on Children's Attitudes Toward Political Authority." *Political Science Quarterly*, 89 (March, 1974), 269-288.

Asher, Herbert. "The Reliability of the Political Efficacy Items." *Political Methodology*, 1 (Spring, 1974), 45-72.

Bachman, Jerald. *Youth in Transition*, Volume 2: *The Impact of Family Background and Intelligence on Tenth-Grade Boys*. Ann Arbor, Michigan: Institute for Social Research, 1970.

Baker, Donald. "Political Socialization: Parameters and Predispositions." *Polity*, 3 (Summer, 1971), 586-600.

Baker, Kendall. "Political Participation, Political Efficacy, and Socialization in Germany." *Comparative Politics*, 6 (October, 1973), 73, 98.

Balch, George. "Multiple Indicators in Survey Research: The Concept Sense of Political Efficacy." *Political Methodology*, 1 (Spring, 1974), 1-43.

Bibliography

Bandura, Albert. *Principles of Behavior Modification.* New York: Holt, Rinehart & Winston, 1969.

Bandura, Albert, Robert Jeffery and Daniel Bachicha. "Analysis of Memory Codes and Cumulative Rehearsal in Observational Learning." *Journal of Research in Personality,* 7 (March, 1974), 295-305.

Barnes, Samuel. "Leadership Style and Political Competence," in Lewis Edinger (ed.), *Political Leadership in Industrialized Societies.* New York: John Wiley and Sons, 1967, 59-83.

Baumol, William J. *Economic Theory and Operations Analysis.* Second edition. Englewood Cliffs: Prentice-Hall, 1965.

Beck, Paul and M. Kent Jennings. "Middle Persons in Political Socialization." *Journal of Politics,* 37 (February, 1975), 83-107.

Bem, Daryl and Andrea Allen. "On Predicting Some of the People Some of the Time: The Search for Cross-Situational Consistencies in Behavior." *Psychological Review,* 81 (November, 1974), 506-520.

Bem, Daryl. "Constructing Cross-Situational Consistencies in Behavior: Some Thoughts on Alker's Critique of Michel." *Journal of Personality,* 40 (1972), 17-26.

Bengston, Vern and M. Lovejoy. "Values, Personality, and Social Structure: An Intergenerational Analysis." *American Behavioral Scientist,* 16 (1973), 880-912.

Bengston, Vern. "Generation and Family Effects in Value Socialization." *American Sociological Review,* 40 (June, 1975), 358-371.

Biederman, Irving, Jan Rabinowitz, Arnold Glass, and E. Webb Stacy, Jr. "On Information Extracted from a Glance at a Scene." *Journal of Experimental Psychology,* 103 (September, 1974), 597-600.

Blalock, Herbert, Jr. *Causal Inferences in Non-experimental Research.* Chapel Hill: University of North Carolina Press, 1961.

Bleda, Paul, Sharon Bleda, Donn Byrne and Leonard White. "When a Bystander Becomes an Accomplice: Situational Determinants of Reactions to Dishonesty." *Journal of Experimental Social Psychology,* 12 (January, 1976), *9-25.*

Bolles, Robert C. "Reinforcement, Expectancy and Learning." *Psychological Review,* 79 (September, 1972), 394-409.

Bowers, Kenneth. "Situationism in Psychology, an Analysis and Critique." *Psychological Review,* 80 (September, 1973), 307-336.

Bowers, William J. "Normative Constraints on Deviant Behavior in the College Context," *Sociometry,* 31 (December, 1968), 370-385.

Brigham, John C. "Racial Stereotypes, Attitudes and Evaluations of and Behavior Intentions Toward Negroes and Whites," *Sociometry*, 34 (September, 1971), 360-380.

Brislin, R. and K. Olmstead. "An Examination of Two Models Designed to Predict Behavior From Attitude and Other Verbal Measures." *Proceedings of the 81st Annual Convention of the American Psychological Association*, 8 (1973), 259-260.

Brunner, Ronald. "Intentionality, Contextuality and Research Methods in the Study of Public Opinion." Paper prepared for the annual meeting of the American Sociological Association. Montreal, Canada, 1974.

Buffalo, M.D. and Joseph W. Rogers. "Behavioral Norms, Moral Norms and Attachment: Problems of Deviance and Conformity." *Social Problems*, 19 (Summer, 1971), 101-113.

Burks, Arthur W. "Cause, Chance and Reason: An Inquiry into the Nature of Scientific Evidence." Unpublished manuscript, 1963.

Burwin, Leroy S. and Donald T. Campbell. "The Generality of Attitudes Toward Authority and Non-Authority Figures." *Journal of Abnormal and Social Psychology*, 54 (1957), 24-31.

Button, Christine. "Political Education for Minority Groups," in Richard Niemi (ed.), *The Politics of Future Citizens*. San Francisco: Jossey Bass, 1974, 167-198.

Button, Christine. "Teaching for Political Efficacy." *Theory into Practise*, 10 (1971), 340-345.

Calder, B. and M. Ross. *Attitudes and Behavior*. New York: General Learning Press, 1973.

Campbell, Angus, Gerald Gurin and Warren Miller. *The Voter Decides*. Evanston, Illinois: Row, Peterson, 1954.

Campbell, Angus, Philip Converse, Warren Miller and Donald Stokes. *The American Voter*. New York: John Wiley, 1960.

Campbell, Donald T. "Social Attitudes and Other Acquired Dispositions," in Sigmund Koch (ed.), *Psychology: A Study of Science*, Volume 6. McGraw Hill, 1964, 159-162.

Campus, Nancy. "Transituational Consistency as a Dimension of Personality." *Journal of Personality and Social Psychology*, 29 (May 1974), 593-600.

Carlson, R. "Where is the Person in Personality Research." *Psychological Bulletin*, 75 (1971), 203-219.

Cartwright, Desmond S. "Trait and Other Sources of Variance in the S-R Inventory of Anxiousness." *Journal of Personality and Social Psychology*, 32 (September, 1975), 408-414.

Castillo, Isidro. "Rural Teacher Training in Mexico," in M.B. Lourenco Filho, *et. al.*, (eds.), *The Training of Rural School Teachers.* UNESCO, Problems of Education, Series 7, 1953.
Chase, William G. and Herbert A. Simon. "The Minds Eye in Chess," in William G. Chase (ed.), *Visual Information Processing.* New York: Academic Press, 1973, 215-281.
Chase, William G. (ed.). *Visual Information Processing.* New York: Academic Press, 1973.
Cherlin, Andrew and Linda Brookover Bourque. "Dimensionality and Reliability of the Rotter I-E Scale." *Sociometry*, 37 (December, 1974), 565-582.
Clarke, Edith. *My Mother Who Fathered Me.* London, England: Allen and Urwin, 1957.
Clausen, Aage R. "Response Validity: Vote Report." *Public Opinion Quarterly*, 32 (Winter, 1968), 588-606.
Cnudde, Charles F. and Donald J. McCrone. "The Linkage Between Constituency Attitudes and Congressional Voting Behavior: A Causal Model." *American Political Science Review*, 60 (March, 1966), 66-72.
Cohen, Arthur R. *Attitude Change and Social Influence.* New York: Basic Books, 1964.
Coie, John, Bruce Pennington, and Hendley Buckley. "Effects of Situational Stress and Sex Roles on the Attribution of Psychological Disorder." *Journal of Consulting and Clinical Psychology*, 42 (August, 1974), 559-568.
Colavita, Francis B. "Human Sensory Dominance," *Perception and Psychophysics*, 16 (October, 1974), 409-412.
Coleman, James S. (ed.). *Education and Political Development.* Princeton: Princeton University Press, 1965.
Coleman, James S. *Introduction to Mathematical Sociology.* Glenco: Free Press, 1964.
Collins, Barry, Joan Martin, Richard Ashmore and Lee Ross. "Some Dimensions of the Internal—External Metaphor in Theories of Personality." *Journal of Personality*, 41 (December, 1973), 471-491.
"Communications to the Editor." *American Political Science Review*, 68 (June, 1975), 720-729.
Connell, R. W. "Political Socialization in the American Family: The Evidence Re-Examined." *Public Opinion Quarterly*, 36 (Fall, 1972), 323-333.
Converse, Philip E. and Georges Dupuex. "Politicization of the Electorate in France and the United States." *Public Opinion Quarterly*, 26 (1962), 1-23.

Converse, Philip. "Attitudes and Non-Attitudes: Continuation of a Dialogue," in Edward Tufte (ed.), *The Quantitative Analysis of Social Problems*. Reading, Mass.: Addison-Wesley, 1970.

Converse, Philip. "Change in the American Electorate," in Angus Campbell and Philip Converse (eds), *The Meaning of Social Change*. New York: Russell Sage, 1972, pp. 263-337.

Converse, Philip. "Of Time and Partisan Stability." *Comparative Political Studies*, 2 (July, 1969), 139-171.

Cook, Thomas and Frank Scioli, Jr. "A Critique of the Learning Concept in Political Socialization Research." *Social Science Quarterly*, 52 (March, 1972), 949-962.

Corning, Peter. "The Biological Basis of Behavior and Some Implications for Political Science." *World Politics*, 23 (April, 1971), 321-370.

Crespi, Irving. "What Kinds of Attitude Measures are Predictors of Behavior?." *Public Opinion Quarterly*, 35 (Fall, 1971), 327-334.

Cundy, Donald. "The Dynamics of Political Attitude Formation: An Empirical Test of a Social Learning Theory." Paper prepared for delivery at the 1976 Annual Meeting of the Midwest Political Science Association, April 29-May 1, 1976.

Dansereau, D. "An Information Processing Model of Mental Multiplication." Unpublished Doctoral Dissertation. Carnegie-Mellon University, 1969.

Diffenbacker, Kenneth and E. Brown. "Memory and Cognition: An Information Processing Model of Man." *Theory and Decision*, 4 (1973), 141-178.

Deffenbacher, Kenneth, Gary Platt and Mark Williams. "Differential Recall as a Function of Socially Induced Arousal and Retention Interval." *Journal of Experimental Psychology*, 103 (October, 1974), 809-811.

Defleur, M. and F. Westie. "Attitude as a Scientific Concept." *Social Forces*, 42 (October, 1963), 17-31.

Defleur, M. and F. Westie. "Verbal Attitudes and Overt Acts." *American Sociological Review*, 23 (December, 1958), 667-673.

Delia, Jesse and Walter Crockett. "Social Schemas, Cognitive Complexity, and the Learning of Social Structures." *Journal of Personality*, 41 (September, 1973), 413-429.

Dennis, Jack. *Political Learning in Childhood and Adolescence: A Study of Fifth, Eighth, and Eleventh Graders in Milwaukee, Wisconsin*. Madison: Wisconsin Research and Development Center for Cognitive Learning, 1969.

Bibliography

Dennis, Jack. "Recent Research on Political Socialization: A Bibliography of Published, Forthcoming, and Unpublished Works, Theses, and Dissertations, and a Survey of Projects in Progress." Prepared for the Theory and Research Working Committee on Political Socialization of the Council on Civic Education. Lincoln Filene Center for Citizenship and Public Affairs, Tufts University, Medford, Massachusetts, 1967.

Deutscher, Irwin. "Words and Deeds: Social Science and Social Policy." *Social Problems*, 13 (Winter, 1966), 235-265.

Dick, A. O. "Iconic Memory and Its Relation to Perceptual Processing and Other Memory Mechanisms." *Perception and Psychophysics*, 16 (December, 1974), 575-596.

Di Palma, Giuseppe and Herbert McClosky. "Personality and Conformity: The Learning of Political Attitudes." *American Political Science Review*, 64 (December, 1970), 1054-1073.

Dowse, Robert and John Hughes. "The Family, the School and the Political Socialization Process." *Sociology*, 5 (January, 1971), 21-45.

Easton, David and Jack Dennis. *Children in the Political System*. New York: McGraw-Hill, 1969.

Easton, David and Jack Dennis. "The Child's Acquisition of Regime Norms: Political Efficacy." *American Political Science Review*, 61 (March, 1967), 25-38.

Edelman, Alexander. *Latin American Politics and Government*. Homewood, Illinois: Dorsey Press, 1965.

Ehman, Lee. "Political Efficacy and the High School Social Studies Curriculum," in Byron G. Massialas (ed.), *Political Youth, Traditional Schools: National and International Perspectives*. Englewood Cliffs, New Jersey: Prentice Hall, 1972, 90-102.

Ekehammar, Bo and David Magnusson. "A Method to Study Stressful Situations." *Journal of Personality and Social Psychology*, 27 (August, 1973), 176-179.

Ekehammar, Bo, Daisy Schalling and David Magnusson. "Dimensions of Stressful Situations: A Comparison Between a Response Analytical and a Stimulus Analytical Approach." *Multivariate Behavioral Research*, 10 (April, 1975), 155-164.

Ekehammar, Bo, David Magnusson and L. Ricklander. "An Interactionist Approach to the Study of Anxiety." *Scandinavian Journal of Psychology*, 15 (1974), 4-14.

Ekhammar, Bo. "Sex Differences in Self-reported Anxiety for Different Situations and Modes of Response." *Scandinavian Journal of Psychology*, 15 (1974), 154-160.

Elder, Glen. *Children of the Great Depression*. Chicago: University of Chicago Press, 1974.

Endler, Norman and J. McV. Hunt. "Generalizability of Contributions from Sources of Variance in the S-R Inventories of Anxiousness." *Journal of Personality*, 37 (March, 1969), 1-24.

Endler, Norman and J. McV. Hunt. "Sources of Behavioral Variance as Measured by the S-R Inventory of Anxiousness." *Psychological Bulletin*, 65 (June, 1966), 336-346.

Endler, Norman and J. McV. Hunt. "S-R Inventories of Hostility and Comparisons of the Proportions of Variance from Persons, Responses, and Situations for Hostility and Anxiousness." *Journal of Personality and Social Psychology*, 9 (August, 1968), 309-315.

Endler, Norman and R. Shedletsky. "Trait versus State Anxiety, Authoritarianism and Ego Threat versus Physical Threat." *Canadian Journal of Behavioral Science*, 5 (1973), 347-361.

Endler, Norman, J. McV. Hunt and A. Rosenstein. "An S-R Inventory of Anxiousness." *Psychological Monographs*, 76 (1962), entire issue.

Endler, Norman. "The Case For Person-Situation Interactions." *Canadian Psychological Review*, 16 (January, 1975), 12-21.

Endler, Norman. "The Person Versus the Situation—A Pseudo Issue? A Response to Alker." *Journal of Personality*, 41 (June, 1973), 287-302.

Escalona, S. "The Differential Impact of Environmental Conditions as a Function of Different Reaction Patterns in Infancy," in J. Westman (ed.), *Individual Differences in Children*. New York: Wiley, 1972.

Estes, William K. "The Cognitive Side of Probability Learning." *Psychological Review*, 83 (January, 1976), 37-64.

Finifter, Ada. "Dimensions of Political Alienation." *American Political Science Review*, 64 (June, 1970), 389-410.

_____, and Abramson, Paul. "City Size and Feelings of Political Competence." *Public Opinion Quarterly*, 39 (Summer, 1975), 189-198.

Fishbein, Martin. "Attitudes and the Prediction of Behavior." *Reading in Attitude Theory and Measurement*. New York: Wiley, 1967, 477-492.

Fishbein, Martin and Icek Ajzen. "Attitudes Towards Objects as Predictors of Single and Multiple Behavioral Criteria." *Psychological Review*, 81 (January, 1974), 59-74.

Flacks, Richard. "The Liberated Generation: An Exploration of the Roots of Student Protest." *Journal of Social Issues*, 23 (July, 1967), 52-72.

Forbes, Hugh D. and Edward R. Tufte. "A Note of Caution in Causal Modelling." *American Political Science Review*, 62 (December, 1968), 1258-1264.

Frederiksen, Carl H. "Effects of Context-Induced Processing Operations on Semantic Information Acquired From Discourse." *Cognitive Psychology*, 7 (April, 1975), 139-166.

Frederiksen, Norman. "Toward a Taxonomy of Situations." *American Psychologist*, 27 (February, 1972), 114-123.

Frideres, J. S., L. G. Warner and S. L. Albrecht. "The Impact of Social Constraints on the Relationship Between Attitudes and Behavior." *Social Forces*, 50 (September, 1971), 102-112.

Gaito, John. *DNA Complex and Adaptive Behavior*. Englewood Cliffs, New Jersey: Prentice-Hall, 1971.

Garcia, F. Chris. "Orientations of Mexican-American and Anglo Children Toward the U. S. Political Community." *Social Science Quarterly*, 53 (March, 1973), 814-829.

Garcia, F. Chris. *The Political Socialization of Chicano Children*. New York: Praeger, 1973.

Garner, Wendell R. *The Processing of Information and Structure*. Potomac, Maryland: Erlbaum, 1974.

Gaudry, Eric, Peter Vagg and Charles Spielberger. "Validation of the State-trait Distinction in Anxiety Research." *Multivariate Behavioral Research*, 10 (July, 1975), 331-342.

Gibson, James J. "Adaption, After-effect and Contrast in the Perception of Curved Lines." *Journal of Experimental Psychology*, 16 (February, 1933), 1-31.

Goldfried, Marvin R. and Ronald Kent. "Traditional Behavioral Personality Assessment: A Comparison of Methodological and Theoretical Assumptions." *Psychological Bulletin*, 77 (June, 1972), 409-420.

Goldrich, Daniel. "Political Organization and the Politicization of the Poblador." *Comparative Political Studies*, 3 (July, 1970), 176-202.

Goslin, David. (ed.). *Handbook of Socialization Theory and Research*. Chicago: Rand McNally, 1969.

Greeley, Andrew. "A Model for Ethnic Political Socialization." *American Journal of Political Science*, 19 (May, 1975), 187-206.

Greenstein, Fred. "Personality and Politics," in Fred Greenstein and Nelson Polsby (eds.), *Handbook of Political Science*, Volume 2. Reading, Massachusetts: Addison-Wesley, 1975, 1-192.

Greenstein, Fred. *Personality and Politics: Problems of Evidence, Inference and Conceptualization*. Chicago: Markham, 1969.

Greenstein, Fred. "The Impact of Personality on Politics: An Attempt to Clear Away the Underbrush." *American Political Science Review*, 61 (September, 1967), 629-641.

_____. "The Standing of Social and Psychological Variables: An Addendum to Jackman's Critique." *Journal of Politics*, 32 (November, 1970), 989-992.

Gustafsson, Gunnel. "Environmental Influence on Political Learning," in Richard Niemi (ed.), *The Politics of Future Citizens*. San Francisco: Jossey Bass, 1974, 166-169.

Haber, Ralph N. "How We Remember What We See," *Scientific American*, 222 (May, 1970) 104-112.

Hagen, Everett. *On the Theory of Social Change*. Homewood, Illinois: The Dorsey Press, 1962.

Hansen, Susan, Linda Franz and Margaret Netemayer-Mays. "Women's Political Participation and Policy Preferences." *Social Science Quarterly*, 56 (March, 1976), 576-590.

Harbison, Frederick and Charles A. Myers. *Education, Manpower and Economic Growth*. New York: McGraw-Hill, 1964.

Harley, George. "Notes on the Poro in Liberia." *Peabody Museum Papers*, Volume 19, No. 2. Cambridge, Massachusetts, 1941.

Harper, Robert J. (ed.). *The Cognitive Processes*. Prentice-Hall, 1964.

Hayden, Teresa and Walter Mischel. "Maintaining Trait Consistency in the Resolution of Behavioral Inconsistency: The Wolf in Sheep's Clothing?." *Journal of Personality*, 44 (March, 1976), 109-132.

Heberlein, Thomas and J. Stanley Black. "Attitudinal Specificity in a Field Setting," *Journal of Personality and Social Psychology*, 33 (April, 1976), 474-479.

Hershey, Margorie Randon and David Hill. "Positional Response Set in Pre-Adult Socialization Surveys." *Social Science Quarterly*, 56 (March, 1976), 707-714.

Hess, Robert and Judith Torney. "The Child's Idealization of Authority." Unpublished manuscript, 1962.

Hess, Robert and Judith Torney. *The Development of Political Attitudes in Children*. Chicago: Aldine, 1967.

Hilgard, Ernst R. *Theories of Learning*. Second edition. New York: Appleton-Century-Crofts, 1956.

Hock, Howard, Gregory Gordon and Robert Whitehurst. "Contextual Relations: The Influence of Familiarity, Physical Plausibility and Belongingness." *Perception and Psycho-Physics*, 16 (August, 1974), 4-8.

Bibliography

Hodges, William and James Felling. "Types of Stressful Situations and Their Relation to Trait Anxiety and Sex." *Journal of Consulting and Clinical Psychology*, 34 (June, 1970), 333-337.

Hoyt, Michael F. "Internal-External Control and Beliefs About Automobile Travel." *Journal of Research in Personality*, (November, 1973), 288-293.

Hulbary, William. "Adolescent Political Self-Images and Political Involvement: The Relative Effects of High School Black Studies Courses and Prior Socialization." Unpublished Ph.D. dissertation, University of Iowa, 1972.

Huttenlocher, Janet and Deborah Burke. "Why Does Memory Span Increase With Age?" *Cognitive Psychology*, 8 (January, 1976), 1-31.

Hyman, Herbert. *Political Socialization*. Glenview, Illinois: Free Press, 1959. Revised edition, 1969.

Inkeles, Alex. "Making Men Modern." *American Journal of Sociology*, 75 (September, 1969), 208-225.

Jaccard, James. "Predicting Social Behavior from Personality Traits." *Journal of Research in Personality*, 7 (March, 1974), 358-367.

Jackman, Robert. "A Note on Intelligence, Social Class, and Political Efficacy in Children." *Journal of Politics*, 32 (November, 1970), 984-989.

Jaros, Dean. *Socialization to Politics*. New York: Praeger, 1973.

Jennings, M. Kent and Richard G. Niemi. "Continuity and Change in Political Orientations: A Longitudinal Study of Two Generations." *American Political Science Review*, 69 (December, 1975), 1316-1335.

Jennings, M. Kent and Richard Niemi. "Patterns of Political Learning." *Harvard Educational Review*, 37 (August, 1968), 443-467.

Jennings, M. Kent and Richard G. Niemi. "The Persistence of Political Orientations: An Over-time Analysis of Two Generations." *British Journal of Political Science*, 8 (July, 1978), 333-363.

Jennings, M. Kent and Richard Niemi. *The Political Character of Adolescence*. Princeton, New Jersey: Princeton University Press, 1974.

Jennings, M. Kent and Richard Niemi. "The Transmission of Political Values From Parents to Child." *American Political Science Review*, 62 (March, 1968), 169-184.

Joe, Victor Clark. "Review of the Internal-External Control Construct as a Personality Variable." *Psychological Reports*, 28 (1971), 619-640.

Jones, Edward and George Goethals. *Order Effects in Impression Formation: Attribution Context and the Nature of the Entity.* New York: General Learning Press, 1971.

Jones, Edward and Richard Nisbett. *The Actor and Observer: Divergent Perceptions of the Causes of Behavior.* New York: General Learning Press, 1971.

Kerr, Madeline. *Personality and Conflict in Jamaica.* Liverpool, England: University Press, 1952.

Kitchen, Helen (ed.). *The Educated African.* New York: Praeger, 1962.

Klemm, W. R. *Science, The Brain and Our Future.* New York: Bobbs-Merrill, 1972.

Klein, Raymond M. and Michael I. Posner. "Attention to Visual and Kinesthetic Components of Skills." *Brain Research*, 71 (1974), 401-411.

Kneller, George F. *The Education of the Mexican Nation.* New York: Columbia University Press, 1951.

Knutson, Jeanne. "Long-term Effects of Personality on Political Attitudes and Beliefs." Paper presented at the annual meeting of the American Political Science Association, New Orleans, 1973.

Knutson, Jeanne. "Personality in the Study of Politics," in Jeanne Knutson (ed.), *Handbook of Political Psychology.* San Francisco: Jossey-Bass, 1973.

Knutson, Jeanne. "Prepolitical Ideologies: The Basis of Political Learning," in Richard Niemi (ed.), *The Politics of Future Citizens.* San Francisco: Jossey-Bass, 1974, 7-40.

Knutson, Jeanne. *The Human Basis of the Polity.* Chicago: Aldine, 1972.

Kornhauser, Arthur, Sheppard, Harold and Albert Mayer. *When Labor Votes: A Study of Auto Workers.* New York: University Books, 1956.

Kothandapani, Virupaksha. "Validation of Feeling, Belief and Intention to Act as Three Components of Attitude and Their Contribution to Prediction of Contraceptive Behavior." *Journal of Personality and Social Psychology*, 19 (September, 1971), 321-333.

Krauss, Ellis S. *Radicals Revisited: A Longitudinal Study of Japanese Student Activists.* Stanford, Cal.: Stanford University Press, 1974.

Krupat, Edward. "Context as a Determinant of Perceived Threat: The Role of Prior Experience." *Journal of Personality and Social Psychology*, 29 (May, 1974), 731-736.

La Berge, D. "Acquisition of Automatic Processing in Perceptual and Associative Learning," in P. M. A. Rabbit and S. Dornic (eds.), *Attention and Performance.* New York: Academic Press, 1975.

Lane, Robert. *Political Life.* Glencoe, Ill.: Free Press, 1959.

Langton, Kenneth P. and David A. Karns. "Political Socialization and National Development: Some Hypotheses and Data." *Western Political Quarterly,* 27 (June, 1974), 217-238.

Langton, Kenneth P. and David A. Karns. "The Relative Influence of Family, Peer Group and School in the Development of Political Efficacy." *Western Political Quarterly,* 22 (December, 1969), 813-826.

Langton, Kenneth P. and M. Kent Jennings. "Political Socialization and the High School Civics Curriculum in the United States." *American Political Science Review,* 62 (September, 1968), 852-867.

Langton, Kenneth P. "Peer Groups and Schools and the Political Socialization Process." *American Political Science Review,* 61 (September, 1967), 751-758.

Langton, Kenneth P. *Political Socialization.* New York: Oxford University Press, 1969.

Langton, Kenneth P. "Situations, Psychological Dispositions and Learning in Understanding the Decision to Participate Politically." Paper delivered at the annual meeting of the American Political Science Association. San Francisco, California, 1975.

La Piere, Richard. "Attitudes Versus Actions." *Social Forces,* 13 (1934), 230-237.

Lasswell, Harold, et. al. *The Comparative Study of Symbols.* Stanford, Cal.: Stanford University Press, 1952.

Le Due, Lawrence. "Measuring the Sense of Political Efficacy in Canada: Problems of Measurement." *Comparative Political Studies,* 8 (October, 1975), 490-495.

Lerner, Daniel. *The Passing of Traditional Society.* New York: Free Press, 1958.

Levenson, Hanna and Jim Miller. "Multidimensional Locus of Control in Sociopolitical Activists of Conservative and Liberal Ideologies." *Journal of Personality and Social Psychology,* 33 (February, 1976), 199-208.

Levine, H. D. and Jean Sicé. "Effects of Set, Setting, and Sedatives on Reaction Time." *Perceptual and Motor Skills,* 42 (April, 1976), 403-412.

Le Vine, Robert A. "Political Socialization and Cultural Change," in Clifford Geertz (ed.), *Old Societies and New States.* New York: Free Press, 1963, 280-303.

Lipset, Seymour and Aldo Solari (eds.). *Elites in Latin America.* New York: Oxford University Press, 1967.

Liska, Alan E. "Attitude-Behavior Consistency as a Function of Generality Equivalence Between Attitude and Behavior Objects." *Journal of Psychology,* 86 (March, 1974), 217-228.

Liska, Alan E. "Emergent Issues in the Attitude-Behavior Consistency Controversy." *American Sociological Review,* 39 (April, 1974), 261-272.

Liska, Alan E. "The Impact of Attitude on Behavior: Attitude—Social Support Interaction." *Pacific Sociological Review,* 17 (January, 1974), 83-91.

Little, Richard. "Mass Political Participation in the U. S. and the USSR: A Conceptual Analysis." *Comparative Political Studies,* 8 (January, 1975), 437-460.

Long, Samuel. "Cognitive-Perceptual Factors in the Political Alienation Process: A Test of Six Models." Paper presented at the 34th Annual Meeting of the Midwest Political Science Association, Chicago, April-May, 1976.

Lyons, Schley. "The Political Socialization of Ghetto Children: Efficacy and Cynicism." *Journal of Politics,* 32 (1970), 288-304.

Magnusson, David. "On Analysis of Situational Dimensions." *Perceptual and Motor Skills,* 32 (June, 1971), 851-867.

Magnusson, David and Bo Ekehammar. "Anxiety Profiles Based on Both Situational and Response Factors." *Multivariate Behavioral Research,* 10 (January, 1975), 27-43.

Magnusson, David and Bo Ekehammar. "An Analysis of Situation Dimensions: A Replication." *Multivariate Behavioral Research,* 8 (July, 1973), 331-339.

Magnusson, David. "The Individual in the Situation: Some Studies on Individuals' Perceptions of Situations." *Studia Psychologica,* 16 (1974), 124-132.

Marsh, David. "Political Socialization: A Critical Review." Ph.D. Dissertation, University of Exeter, England, 1973.

Marsh, David. "Political Socialization and Intergenerational Stability in Political Attitudes." *British Journal of Political Science,* 5 (October, 1975), 509-515.

Marsh, David. "Political Socialization, the Implicit Assumptions Questioned." *British Journal of Political Science,* 1 (October, 1971), 453-465.

Marvick, Dwaine. "African University Students: A Presumptive Elite," in James S. Coleman (ed.), *Education and Political Development.* Princeton: Princeton University Press, 1965, 463-497.

Matheny, Adam P., Jr. and Anne Brown Dolan. "Persons, Situations, and Time: A Genetic View of Behavioral Change in Children." *Journal of Personality and Social Psychology*, 32 (December, 1975), 1106-1110.

McCall, Raymond. "Beyond Reason and Evidence: The Metapsychology of Professor B. F. Skinner." *Journal of Clinical Psychology*, 28 (April, 1972), 125-139.

McClelland, David. *The Achieving Society*. New York: Van Nostrand, 1961.

McPherson, J. Miller, Susan Welch and Cal Clark. "The Stability and Reliability of Political Efficacy: Using Path Analysis to Test Alternative Models." *American Political Science Review*, 71 (June, 1977), 509-521.

Merelman, Richard. *Political Socialization and Educational Climates: A Study of Two School Districts*. New York: Holt, Rinehart, and Winston, 1971.

Merelman, Richard. "Public Education and Social Structure: Three Modes of Adjustment." *Journal of Politics*, 35 (November, 1973), 798-829.

Merelman, Richard. "The Adolescence of Political Socialization." *Sociology of Education*, 45 (1972), 134-166.

Merelman, Richard. "The Development of Policy Thinking in Adolescence." *American Political Science Review*, 65 (December, 1971), 1033-1047.

Merelman, Richard. "The Structure of Policy Thinking in Adolescence: A Research Note." *American Political Science Review*, 67 (March, 1973), 161-168.

Mikulas, William. *Behavior Modification: An Overview*. New York: Harper and Row, 1972.

Milbrath, Lester. *Political Participation*. Chicago: Rand McNally, 1965.

Miller, Arthur. "Political Issues and Trust in Government: 1964-1970." *American Political Science Review*, 68 (September, 1974), 951-972.

Miller, Arthur, Thad Brown and Alden Raine. "Social Conflict and Political Estrangement." Paper delivered at the annual meeting of the Midwest Political Science Association. Chicago, Illinois, May, 1973.

Miller, Daniel R. and Guy E. Swanson. *The Changing American Parent*. New York: Wiley, 1958.

Miller, Norman and Donald T. Campbell. "Recency and Primacy in Persuasion as a Function of the Timing of Speeches and Measurements." *Journal of Abnormal and Social Psychology*, 59 (1959), 1-9.

Miller, Warren E. and Donald E. Stokes. "Constituency Influence in Congress," *American Political Science Review*, 57 (March, 1963), 45-56.

Mischel, Walter. "Continuity and Change in Personality." *American Psychologist*, 24 (1969), 1002-1018.

Mischel, Walter. *Introduction To Personality*. Second edition. New Your: Holt, Rinehart and Winston, 1976.

Mischel, Walter. "On the Empirical Dilemmas of Psychodynamic Approaches: Issues and Alternatives," *Journal of Abnormal Psychology*, 74 (1973), 252-283.

Mischel, Walter. *Personality and Assessment*. New York: Wiley, 1968.

Mischel, Walter. "Toward a Cognitive Social Learning Reconceptualization of Personality." *Psychological Review*, 80 (July, 1973), 252-283.

Moos, Rudolf. "Conceptualization of Human Environment." *American Psychologist*, 28 (August, 1973), 652-665.

Moos, Rudolf. "Differential Effects of Psychiatric Ward Settings on Patient Change." *Journal of Nervous and Mental Disease*, 5 (1970), 316-321.

Moos, Rudolf. "Situational Analysis of a Therapeutic Community Milieu." *Journal of Abnormal Psychology*, 73 (February, 1968), 49-61.

Moos, Rudolf. "Sources of Variance in Responses to Questionnaires and in Behavior," *Journal of Abnormal Psychology*, 74 (1969), 405-412.

Morgan, Jan. "Women and Political Socialization: Fact and Fantasy in Easton and Dennis, and in Lane." *Politics*, 9 (May, 1974), 50-55.

Muller, Edward. "Cross-National Dimensions of Political Competence." *American Political Science Review*, 64 (September, 1970), 792-809.

Natsoulas, Thomas. "The Subjective, Experimental Element in Perception." *Psychological Bulletin*, 81 (October, 1974), 611-631.

Nesbett, Richard and Linda Temoshok. "Is There An 'External' Cognitive Style?" *Journal of Personality and Social Psychology*, 33 (January, 1976), 36-47.

Newcomb, Theodore M. *Persistence and Change*. New York: Wiley, 1967.

Newell, Allen and Herbert Simon. *Human Problem Solving*. Englewood Cliffs, New Jersey: Prentice-Hall, 1972.

Newell, Allen. "A Theoretical Exploration of Mechanisms for Coding the Stimulus," in A. W. Melton and E. Martin (eds.), *Coding Processes in Human Memory*. Washington, D. C.: Winston, 1972.

Neisser, Ulric and Robert Becklen. "Selective Looking: Attending to Visually Specified Events." *Cognitive Psychology*, 7 (October, 1975), 480-494.

Neisser, Ulric. *Cognitive Psychology*. New York: Appleton-Century-Crofts, 1967.

Nie, Norman H., G. Bingham Powell, Jr., and Kenneth Prewitt. "Social Structure and Political Participation: Developmental Relationships." *American Political Science Review*, 63 (June, 1969), 361-378 and 63 (September, 1969), 808-832.

Niemi, Richard. "A Methodological Study of Political Socialization in the Family." Ph.D. Dissertation, University of Michigan, Department of Political Science, 1967.

Nurulla, Syed and J. P. Nalik. *A History of Education in India*. Bombay, India: MacMillan, 1951.

Orum, Anthony and Roberta Cohen. "The Development of Political Orientations Among Black and White Children." *American Sociological Review*, 38 (February, 1973), 62-73.

Orum, Anthony, Roberta Cohen, Sherri Grasmuek and Amy Orum. "Sex, Socialization and Politics." *American Sociological Review*, 39 (April, 1974), 197-209.

Osgood, Charles. "Toward a Wedding of Insufficiencies," in Theodore Dixon and David Osgood (eds.), *Verbal Behavior and General Behavior Theory*. Englewood Cliffs, New Jersey: Prentice Hall, 1968, 495-519.

Overton, W. "On the Assumptive Base of the Nature-Nurture Controversy: Additive versus Interactive Conceptions." *Human Development*, 16 (1973), 74-89.

Patella, Victoria and William Kuvlesky. "Situational Variation in Language Patterns of Mexican-American Boys and Girls." *Social Science Quarterly*, 53 (March, 1973), 855-864.

Patrick, John J. "Political Socialization of American Youth: A Review of Research With Implications for Secondary School Social Studies." High School Curriculum Center in Government, Indiana University, Bloomington, Indiana, 1967.

Peterson, Donald R. *The Clinical Study of Social Behavior*. New York: Appleton-Century-Crofts, 1968.

Philipps, Derek L. *Knowledge From What*. Chicago: Rand McNally, 1971.

Phillips, W. A. "On the Distinction Between Sensory Storage and Short-Term Visual Memory." *Perception and Psycho-Physics*, 16 (October, 1974), 283-290.

Pinard, Maurice, Jerome Kirk and Donald Von Eschen. "Process of Recruitment in the Sit-in Movement." *Public Opinion Quarterly*, 33 (Fall, 1969), 355-369.

Posner, Michael I., Mary Jo Nissen and Raymond M. Klein. "Visual Dominance: An Information-Processing Account of Its Origins and Significance." *Psychological Review*, 83 (March, 1976), 157-171.

Posner, Michael I. "Psycho-biology of Attention," in M. Gazzaniga and C. Blakemore (eds.), *Handbook of Psychobiology*. New York: Academic Press, 1975.

Prewitt, Kenneth. "Political Efficacy," in David Sills (ed.), *International Encyclopedia of the Social Sciences*. New York: Crowell, Collier, and Macmillan, 1968, 225-228.

Rausch, H., I. Farbman and L. Llewellyn. "Person, Setting and Change in Social Interaction: II. A Normal Control Study." *Human Relations*, 13 (1960), 305-332.

Renshon, Stanley. *Psychological Needs and Political Behavior: A Theory of Personality and Political Efficacy*. New York: Free Press, 1974.

Renshon, Stanley. "The Psychological Origins of Political Efficacy: The Need for Personal Control." Paper delivered at the Annual Meeting of the American Political Science Association. Washington, D. C., 1972.

—————. "The Role of Personality Development in Political Socialization," in David Schwartz and Sandra Kenyon Schwartz (eds.), *New Directions in Political Socialization*. New York: Free Press, 1975, 29-68.

Riccards, Michael. *The Making of the American Citizenry: An Introduction to Political Socialization*. New York: Chandler, 1973.

Ringuette, Eugene. "The Stability of Individual Differences in Behavior Across Experimental Conflict Situations." *Journal of Research in Personality*, 10 (June, 1976), 177-182.

Rodgers, Harrell, Jr. "Toward Exploration of the Political Efficacy and Political Cynicism of Black Adolescents: An Explanatory Study." *American Journal of Political Science*, 18 (May, 1974), 257-282.

Rohter, Ira. "A Social-Learning Approach to Political Socialization," in David Schwartz and Sandra Kenyon Schwartz (eds.), *New Directions in Political Socialization*. New York: Free Press, 129-162.

Rokeach, Milton and P. Kliejunas. "Behavior as a Function of Attitude-toward-Object and Attitude-toward-Situation." *Journal of Personality and Social Psychology*, 22 (May, 1972), 194-201.

Rokeach, Milton. *Beliefs, Attitudes and Values.* San Francisco: Jossey-Bass, 1968.

Rosenbaum, James. "The Stratification of Socialization Processes." *American Sociological Review*, 40 (February, 1975), 48-54.

Rosenberg, Morris, "The Logical Status of Suppressor Variables." *Public Opinion Quarterly*, 37 (Fall, 1973), 359-372.

Rotter, J. B. "Generalized Expectancies for Internal Versus External Control of Reinforcement." *Psychological Monographs*, 80 (1966), entire issue of No. 609.

Salisbury, Robert. "Research on Political Participation." *American Journal of Political Science*, 19 (May, 1975), 323-342.

Sanger, Susan Phipps and Henry A. Alker. "Dimensions of Internal-External Locus of Control and the Women's Liberation Movement." *Journal of Social Issues*, 28 (1972), 115-129.

Schonfield, William. "The Focus of Socialization Research: An Evaluation." *World Politics*, 23 (April, 1971), 544-578.

Schuman, Howard and Jean Converse. "The Effects of Black and White Interviewers on Black Responses in 1968." *Public Opinion Quarterly*, 35 (Spring, 1971), 44-68.

Seaman, Jerrol and Frederick Koenig. "A Comparison of Measures of Cognitive Complexity." *Sociometry*, 37 (September, 1974), 375-390.

Searing, Donald, Gerald Wright and George Robinowitz. "The Primacy Principle: Attitude Change and Political Socialization." *British Journal of Political Science*, 6 (January, 1976), 83-113.

Sears, David. "Book Review." *Midwest Journal of Political Science*, 15 (February, 1971), 156.

_____. *Political Attitudes Through the Life Cycle.* San Francisco: Freeman, forthcoming.

_____. "Political Socialization," in Fred Greenstein and Nelson Polsby (eds.), *Handbook of Political Science, Volume 2: Micropolitical Theory.* Reading, Mass.: Addison-Wesley, 1975, 93-153.

Seligman, Martin. "On the Generality of the Laws of Learning." *Psychological Review*, 77 (September, 1970) 406-418.

Schneider, David J. "Implicit Personality Theory: A Review." *Psychological Bulletin*, 79 (May, 1973), 294-309.

Schonfeld, William R. "The Focus of Political Socialization Research: An Evaluation." *World Politics*, 23 (April, 1971), 544-578.

Schuman, Howard. "Attitudes vs. Actions Versus Attitudes vs. Attitudes." *Public Opinion Quarterly*, 36 (Fall, 1972), 347-354.

Schweder, Richard. "How Relevant Is an Individual Difference Theory of Personality." *Journal of Personality*, 43 (September, 1975), 455-484.

Scioli, Frank, Jr. and James Dyson. "Attitude—Behavior Congruence in Varying Situational Environments." *Experimental Study of Politics*, 2 (March, 1973), 39-60.

Shallice, Tim. "On the Dual Functions of Consciousness." *Psychological Review*, 79 (September, 1972), 383-390.

Sherman, S. J. "Internal-External Control and Its Relationship to Attitude Change Under Different Social Influence Techniques." *Journal of Personality and Social Psychology*, 26 (1973), 23-29.

Sigel, Roberta. *Adolescence and Political Involvement*. North Scituate, Mass.: Duxbury Press, 1973.

_____. "Psychological Antecedents and Political Involvement: The Utility of the Concept of Locus-of-Control." *Social Science Quarterly*, 56 (September, 1975), 315-323.

Silvern, Louise. "The Effect of Traditional vs. Counter-Culture Attitudes on the Relationship Between the Internal-External Scale and Political Position." *Journal of Personality*, 43 (March, 1975), 58-73.

Simon, Herbert A. and Michael Barenfeld. "Information Processing Analysis of Perceptual Processes in Problem Solving." *Psychological Review*, 76 (September, 1969), 473-483.

Simon, Herbert A. *Models of Man*. New York: Wiley, 1957.

Simon, Herbert A. "The Functional Equivalence of Problem Solving Skills." *Cognitive Psychology*, 7 (April, 1975), 268-288.

Simon, Herbert A. *The Sciences of the Artificial*. Cambridge: MIT Press, 1969.

Skinner, Burrhus F. *Beyond Freedom and Dignity*. New York: Knopf, 1971.

Smith, M. Brewster. "Competence and Socialization," in John A. Clausen (ed.), *Socialization and Society*. Boston: Little, Brown, 1968, 271-320.

Sniderman, Paul. *Personality and Democratic Politics*. Berkeley: University of California Press, 1975.

Snyder, Melvin and Edward Jones. "Attitude Attribution When Behavior Is Constrained." *Journal of Experimental Social Psychology*, 10 (November, 1974), 585-600.

Songer, Elaine. "The Importance of Situational Factors: An Examination and Extension of the Fishbein Model." Unpublished Doctoral Dissertation, University of North Carolina, 1973.

Songer-Nocks, Elaine. "Situational Factors Affecting the Weighting of Predictor Components in the Fishbein Model." *Journal of Experimental Social Psychology*, 12 (January, 1976), 56-69.

Sonquist, John, Elizabeth Lanh Baker and James Morgan. *Searching for Structure*. Ann Arbor, Michigan: Institute for Social Research, University of Michigan, 1973.

Staats, Arthur. *Social Behaviorism*. Homewood, Illinois: Dorsey, 1975.

Stillman, Peter. "The Limits of Behaviorism: A Review Essay on B. F. Skinners' Social and Political Thought." *American Political Science*, 69 (March, 1975), 202-213.

Stone, William. *The Psychology of Politics*. New York: Free Press, 1974.

Tapper, Ted. *Political Education and Stability: Elite Responses to Political Conflict*. New York: Wiley, 1976.

Tedin, Kent L. "The Influence of Parents on the Political Attitudes of Adolescents." *American Political Science Review*, 68 (December, 1974), 1579-1592.

Thalheimer, Ross. *Reflections: Bio-Psychological, Psychoanalytic, Socio-Political, Aesthetic and Personal*. New York: Philosophical Library, 1972.

Theil, Henri. *Principles of Econometrics*. New York: Wiley, 1971.

Throop, Warren and A. P. MacDonald, Jr. "Internal-External Locus of Control: A Bibliography." *Psychological Reports* 28 (1971), 175-190.

Tittle, Charles and Richard Hill. "The Accuracy of Self-Reported Data and Prediction of Political Activity," *Public Opinion Quarterly*, 31 (Spring, 1967), 103-106.

Thomas, Ewart and Wanda Weaver. "Cognitive Processing and Time Perception." *Perception and Psychophysics*, 17 (April, 1975), 363-367.

Tolley, Howard, Jr. *Children and War*. New York: Teachers College Press, 1973.

Torgerson, Warren. *Theory and Methods of Scaling*. New York: Wiley, 1963.

UNESCO, *World Survey of Education, II: Primary Education*. Paris, 1958.

United Nations, *The Economic Development of Latin America in the Post-War Period*, 1964.

Vaillancourt, Pauline. "Stability of Children's Survey Responses." *Public Opinion Quarterly*, 37 (Fall, 1973), 373-387.

Vaizey, John. "Economics of Education." *International Social Science Journal*, 14 (1962), 627.

Verba, Sidney and Norman Nie. *Participation in America: Political Democracy and Social Equality*. New York: Harper and Row, 1972.

Wallach, Michael A. and Margaret I. Leggett. "Testing the Hypothesis That a Person Will be Consistent: Stylistic Consistency Versus Situational Specificity in Size of Children's Drawings." *Journal of Personality*, 40 (September, 1972), 309-330.

Warner, Lyle and M. Defleur. "Attitude as an Interactional Concept: Social Constraint and Social Distance as Intervening Variables Between Attitudes and Action." *American Sociological Review*, 34 (April, 1967), 153-169.

Washburn, Philo. "Authoritarianism and Political Participation." *Journal of Political and Military Sociology*, 3 (Fall, 1975), 165-178.

Watts, Meredith. "B. F. Skinner and the Technological Control of Social Behavior." *American Political Science Review*, 69 (March, 1975), 214-227.

Watts, Meredith. "Efficacy, Trust and Commitment to the Political Process." *Social Science Quarterly*, 54 (December, 1973), 623-631.

Weinstein, Alan G. "Predicting Behavior from Attitudes." *Public Opinion Quarterly*, 36 (Fall, 1972), 355-360.

Weissberg, Robert. *Political Choice and Democratic Citizenship*. Englewood Cliffs, New Jersey: Prentice-Hall, 1974.

_____. "Political Efficacy and Political Allusion." *Journal of Politics*, 37 (May, 1975), 469-487.

_____. *Political Learning, Political Choice, and Democratic Citizenship*. Englewood Cliffs, New Jersey: Prentice-Hall, 1974.

_____ and Richard Joslyn. "Methodological Appropriateness in Political Socialization Research," in Stanley Renshon (ed.), *Handbook of Political Socialization: Theory and Research*. New York: Free Press, Forthcoming.

Welch, Susan and Cal Clark. "Determinants of Change in Political Efficacy: A Test of Two Hypotheses." *Journal of Political and Military Sociology*, 3 (Fall, 1975), 207-218.

Wheeler, Stanton and Orville Brim. *Socialization After Childhood: Two Essays*. New York: Wiley, 1966.

White, Elliot. "Intelligence and Sense of Political Efficacy in Children." *Journal of Politics*, 30 (August, 1968), 710-732.

White, Glenn M. "Contextual Determinants of Opinion Judgments: Field Experimental Probes of Judgmental Relativity Boundary Conditions." *Journal of Personality and Social Psychology*, 32 (December, 1975), 1047-1054.

Wicker, Allen W., "An Examination of the Other Variables' Explanation of Attitude—Behavior Inconsistency." *Journal of Personality and Social Psychology*, 19 (July, 1971), 18-30.

Wicker, Allen W. and R. J. Pomazal. "The Relationship Between Attitudes and Behavior as a Function of Specificity of Attitude Object and Presence of a Significant Person During Assessment Conditions." *Representative Research in Social Psychology*, 2 (July, 1971), 26-31.

Wicker, Allen W. "Attitude Versus Actions: The Relatioship of Verbal and Overt Behavioral Responses to Attitude Objects." *Journal of Social Issues*, 25 (Autumn, 1969), 41-78.

Wilson, Stephan and Larry A. Benner. "The Effects of Self-Esteem and Situation upon Comparison Choices During Ability Evaluation." *Sociometry*, 34 (September, 1971), 381-397.

Wonnacott, Ronald J. and Thomas H. Wonnacott. *Econometrics*. New York: Wiley, 1970.

Wright, James. "Political Socialization Research: the 'Primacy' Principle." *Social Forces*, 53 (June, 1975), 243-256.

Wright, Sewall. "Correlation and Causation." *Journal of Agricultural Research*, 20 (January, 1921), 557-585.

Wright, Sewall. "The Interpretation of Multivariate Systems," in O. Kempthorne, et. al., *Statistics and Mathematics in Biology*. Ames: Iowa State College Press, 1954, pp. 11-33.

Zadeck, S. "Problems with the Use of 'Moderator' Variables." *Psychological Bulletin*, 76 (1971), 295-310.

Zajonc, Robert. "Cognitive Theories in Social Psychology," in G. Lindzey and E. Aronson (eds.), the Handbook of *Social Psychology*, Volume 1. Reading, Massachusetts: Addison-Wesley, 1968, 320-411.

INDEX

Allport and Odbert
  trait-like words, 21
Almond and Verba
  socialization agents in five nations, 38
  study on five nations, 42
Automatic Interaction Detector and Program (AID), defined, 92

Bem and Allen
  variability of efficacy, 136
Bolles, Robert C.
  animal learning, 22
Bowers, Kenneth
  written description vs. natural setting, 75

Campbell, Angus
  theory of political efficacy, 19
Campbell, Gurin and Miller
  measurement of political efficacy, 18
Childhood
  effects on politization, 28-29
Clarke, Edith
  family ties, 41
Cognitive processing, 131-133
Cognitive processing approach
  outlined, 24
Cognitive sensitivity, 102-103
Cohen, Arthur
  learning retention, 50
Converse, Philip
  early learning and political efficacy, 39
Crespi, Irving
  situational dynamics, 114
Criterion of behavior, 113-115

Decision to participate in politics
  behavior intention vs. participation, 99-101
Dispositions
  effect on political participation, 17-20
  organizers of human behavior, 18
  situational influence on, 21

Early learning
  primacy of, 37-39
  effect on political efficacy, 60
Education
  effect on family life, 41
Efficacy questions
  defined, 25
Efficacy score
  defined, 26
Endler and Hunt
  psychological tendencies, 136
Experience of others
  influential, 24
External factors
  influence on behavior, 21

Family, school, work experience
  influence on political efficacy, 49-51
Fishbein and Ajzen
  relationship between attitude and behavior, 113
Four predictors of situational efficacy, 92-96

General political efficacy
  function of, 75
  minimization of, 75
Generalizing
  decision-making, 22
Global attitudes
  stability of, 24

Goldrich, Daniel
  pobladores, 24, 26
Great Britain
  work environment, 60
Guttman scales
  respondents perceived efficacy, 42

Individual vs. collective action, 86
Industrialization
  influence on family, 41
  links to employment, 57

Jennings and Niemi
  correlation between efficacy and participation, 19
  internal political efficacy, 39
  personality change, 128
  political link between parents and children, 37
  sample findings, 38

Labeling
  personality, 21
Lane, Robert E.
  theory of political efficacy, 18, 19
Langton, Kenneth P.
  theory of politization as catalyst, 19
Langton and Karns
  attitudes of Jamaican adolescents, 38
Learning
  cognitive, 22
  prior situational, 17
Likert scale
  five points, 76
Liska, Alan
  relationship between attitude and behavior, 99-100

MANOVA
  defined, 92-93
Moderator variables, 116-124
Moderator variables and social class, 136-138
Moos, Rudolf
  psychological tendencies, 136
  situations' impact on behavior, 103

Nie, Powell and Prewitt
  political efficacy correlated with political participation, 24

Non-linearity
  of participation in politics, 51-52

Organizational settings and political experience, 138-139
Osgood, Charles
  explanations of performance, 20
Others' influence on political activity, 92

Participation in politics
  antecedents for, 17
  antecedents to, 18
  factors influencing, 28
  five predictors and their interaction, 101-113
  participation in politics response to stimulation, 22
  predictors or variables for, 17
Personality vs. situations, 134-136
Pobladores
  political activism of, 26-28
Political efficacy
  confidence, 20
  correlated with education, 39
  correlation to political participation, 24
  early learning, 30
  ego strength and politization, 19
  function of, 75
  global psychological disposition, 20
  personality traits for, 18
  predictor for political participation, 19
  stable disposition, 19
  stability of, 19
  stability over time, 83-84
Political stability and ego strength, 19
Posner, Nissen, and Klein
  visual stimuli, 132-133
Predictors
  contribution of, 112
Primacy
  of early learning, 37
Primacy effect
  defined, 21
Prior learning
  impact on politization, 17
Priorities and "rational" decisions, 120-124
Psychodynamic links to political behavior, 127-129

Index

Psychodynamic assumptions
  defined, 29
  findings for, 60
Psychodynamic model, 29

Questionnaire
  on political efficacy, 69

Rational Decisions to participate, 130
Relative contribution of predictors, 112-113
Relative influence of job and family on political efficacy, 42
Renshon, Stanley
  inconsistencies in subjects' behavior, 24
  need for control, 19

Sample characteristics, 71-72
Sample questions
  questionnaire on political efficacy, 70-71
Searing, Wright and Rabinowitz
  instability of political efficacy, 38-39
Sexual Differentiation, 118-120
Situation
  stimulus for response, 20-21

Situation — specific beliefs
  influence on political participation, 17
Situation vs. cognition, 20-21
Situational link to political behavior, 129
Situational efficacy
  interaction between four predictors, 92-96
Situations
  effects on political participation, 17
Socialization
  impact of, on political efficacy, 40
Socialization agents, 133-134
  and National Development, 39-40
  effect of, 55-56

Test for political activity, 68-71
Typing
  individual, 21

Unstructured Situations, 114-115

Variables and Measurements
  for testing, 42
Vietnam War
  political activists in, 68